DATE DUE			
MAY 18 '70			

POLITICAL POWER
AND SOCIAL THEORY

POLITICAL POWER
AND SOCIAL THEORY

SIX STUDIES

BARRINGTON MOORE, Jr.

HARVARD UNIVERSITY PRESS

Cambridge, Massachusetts

1958

Distributed in Great Britain by
Oxford University Press
London

Publication of this book was aided by a grant
from the Ford Foundation.

Library of Congress Catalog Card Number 58–11553

Printed in the United States of America

To E. C. M.

PREFACE

The papers in this little volume represent a series of attempts to find answers for questions that have interested or disturbed me in the course of more sustained research on the nature of politics in modern industrial society. They reflect concern with three closely related problems.

The first problem may be put in these words: to what extent can one make valid generalizations about politics, or indeed any aspect of society, without being merely trite and pompous? Demonstration by example gives the best answer to this question, though I do not flatter myself in thinking that my answers are completely satisfactory. The book begins, therefore, with two straightforward factual studies. The first analyzes certain recurring processes in the acquisition of power. The second discusses those aspects of modern totalitarianism that also occur in the pre-industrial world.

The second problem concerns the limitations and possibilities of a generalizing science, or series of sciences, based on the models of natural science, for intelligent understanding of human affairs. The next two essays attempt to assess some modern trends in this endeavor, as well as some older ones that have fallen into disfavor. While I have tried to give some grounds for holding that some of the older views deserve far more serious consideration than they receive at present, I do not take an anachronistic stand for its own sake. Instead, I have done my best to discern what there may be of value and promise, both in contemporary practice and in older traditions. The mutual contempt that many scholars from the humanist tradition and the newer social sciences feel for one another merely tends to throw false issues into the foreground. There is no real reason why one cannot discuss issues important to the humanist with scientific care and attention to the evidence.

The last two essays take up, through concrete examples, the problem of estimating current social trends with an eye to the future. I do not believe it is possible to make detailed predictions about human society, except perhaps on a short-run basis and then, as a rule, about rather limited problems. On the other hand, I think it is possible, at least in principle, to indicate the range of alternatives, in their broad structural outlines, within which variation may occur, as well as the costs to be expected from different courses of action. Many people today would probably agree that historical situations are seldom either completely open or completely closed. The real problems arise as soon as one tries to be specific.

My views on all these questions have changed gradually over the years. I have therefore revised two of the essays that have appeared before in print, "Notes on the Process of Acquiring Power" and "The New Scholasticism and the Study of Politics" (*World Politics,* vol. VIII, no. 1 [October, 1955], pp. 1–19, and vol. VI, no. 1 [October, 1953], pp. 122–138, respectively). My thanks are due to the publishers of *World Politics* for permission to reprint these papers, as well as to those of the *American Journal of So-*

ciology for permission to use a few sentences from my "Sociological Theory and Contemporary Politics" (vol. LXI, no. 2 [September, 1955], pp. 107–115). The other four essays in this book are published here for the first time.

A word on style may be appropriate in this preface. Though the species may be on the decline, I continue to hope that a few specimens of the general reader — the person interested in following the discussion of important problems without seeking professional competence in their solution — may still exist among the speakers of the English language. I have therefore tried as far as possible to write in this language. The editorial "we" I have generally avoided, as well as circumlocutions in the passive voice, since both forms are not only clumsy but confer an unwarranted aura of authority, suggesting a united body of professional opinion behind statements made in this way. Where the expression "we" does occur, it refers to the reader as a companion in the search for truth. The freedom provided by the essay's form I have used to explore certain problems beyond the point where definite answers are possible. At the same time I have tried to indicate the strength of the arguments both by the choice of wording and by documentary references in the tradition of responsible scholarship. For the sake of the general reader too, as well as on account of the economics of publishing, all such references and discussions of interest only to specialists have been relegated to the back of the book. A few footnotes important to the understanding of the text appear at the bottom of the page.

The publication of these essays provides me with a welcome opportunity to express publicly my thanks to a very good friend, Professor Herbert Marcuse of Brandeis University. From him I have learned a great deal about philosophy and the study of history. Some of the papers in this book are in substantial measure the outcome of conversations with him. It is mainly through these vigorous discussions that I have in recent years experienced the tremendous excitement that intellectual pursuits should sometimes produce if they are to be worthwhile.

Many other persons have also given me important help. Professor William L. Langer, Director of the Russian Research Center, and Mr. Marshall D. Shulman, Associate Director, have given me steadfast encouragement and provided the rare privilege of time to be spent wholly on research during a large part of each academic year. In this way they have enabled me to attack problems that would otherwise have been even more beyond my powers. These essays, composed largely in vacation hours that could not always be devoted to the main task, are no more than a by-product of their efforts on my behalf. Some day they may have a more tangible reward.

Through discussion at seminars and through their comments on specific points the following colleagues have given very real assistance: Robert N. Bellah, Alexander Eckstein, John K. Fairbank, Robert A. Feldmesser, Carl J. Friedrich, Clyde K. M. Kluckhohn, Daniel H. H. Ingalls, Alex Inkeles, Talcott Parsons, David M. Schneider, Samuel A. Stouffer, and Robert L. Wolff. With so much good advice, there is scarcely any excuse for the faults that remain. Elizabeth C. Moore, whose affectionate yet firm prods in the interests of clarity are an indispensable part of everything I write, knows full well where the remaining trouble lies. Some day I hope to write a book that is up to her standards.

Alta, Utah
January, 1958

BARRINGTON MOORE, JR.

CONTENTS

POLITICAL POWER
AND SOCIAL THEORY

· 1 ·

NOTES ON THE PROCESS
OF ACQUIRING POWER

Hundreds of books have been written to describe the ways in which particular groups or individuals have come to exercise domination over large numbers of their fellows. Despite this tempting wealth of factual material, or perhaps because of it, modern social science has very largely avoided any attempt to discover and explain, within a strictly empirical framework, what recurring patterns there may be in these myriads of events. The following pages represent a very modest effort in this direction.

If there is indeed a distinguishable process of acquiring power, or, as is more likely, a series of such processes, the attempt to distinguish them must be formulated in terms of a time sequence. It should indicate the conditions in the society as a whole that lead to a concentration of power. In addition, it should indicate the sequence of stages through which the concentration takes place.

There is of course no need to adopt a priori the view that all societies pass through absolutely identical or even closely similar stages whenever power becomes concentrated. A more fruitful approach may be to try to analyze the range of problems encountered by different types of social groups on the road to power, and the variety of solutions they have attempted at each stage of the journey. Though what I have to say is concerned primarily with the acquisition of power and authority over an entire society, many of these observations apply also to the acquisition of domination over smaller groupings. The establishment of a new and vigorous administration in a corporation, a university, or a labor union displays recognizable similarities to corresponding phenomena in society as a whole.

The first question that occurs rather naturally is how the power-seeking process begins. Are there, for example, any common features in the situations that start the Bolsheviks on the way to the Kremlin, the early Christians on the route that leads to Innocent III, the French kings on the road to Versailles, the Moguls on the way to the splendors of Shah Jahan's reign? Here we may limit our attention to some of the grosser structural features of the societies that nourish the seekers after power.

There are, I suggest, at least three main types of situations that serve to initiate an active search for political power and political centralization. The first and simplest is the case in which a society undertakes some new set of activities that by their very nature require a high degree of central coordination. A second and much more complex case occurs when either external shock or internal decay produces a movement for the forced reintegration of a society around new or partially new patterns of behavior. The third type, for which the somewhat unsatisfactory term "monarchical absolutism" may be offered, is found where the rulers of one segment of a loosely ordered system gradually expand their control over the whole system or a substantial part of it. Perhaps none of these generalized causal antecedents ever occur in a completely pure form. Certainly cases can be found where all of these factors are intertwined with one another. Yet each of the three is at least analytically distinguishable, and empirical approximations may be found in the record of history.

Among the new activities requiring a high degree of central coordination, the emergence of warfare on a large scale provides one of the clearest examples. The development of irrigation systems on a broad territorial base is another. Marx, and some who follow in his footsteps, have regarded this factor as the major one behind the growth of Oriental despotisms.[1] The growth of modern industry provides still another illustration. Though recent research has thrown some doubt upon the thesis that increasing monopoly characterizes industrial advance,[2] the expanding role of the central government over the past fifty years can scarcely be denied.

What is it about such new activities, which evidently are not limited to modern industrial society, that bring about great concentrations of power? In the illustrations that have been offered three general characteristics may be observed. In the first place, the activity in each case calls for the allocation of large amounts of human and natural resources. The allocation is a continuous process that requires frequent changes of direction. This is particularly true of a military organization, in which large bodies of men and materials may have to be shifted rapidly from one place to another in accord with swiftly changing circumstances. Likewise, when industry fails to flow in the directions deemed socially desirable, the pressure for political control rises. In the second place, each activity is one in which large numbers of people have to be persuaded or compelled to act against their earlier habits and perhaps even their natural inclinations. One recalls the effort of disciplining the labor force that has accompanied modern industrialization, as well as its sterner counterparts in military organizations and the great public works of Oriental despotism. Finally, in each activity a competitive advantage accrues to that social unit which can mobilize or control the larger quantity of resources. Up to a limit in size that cannot be specified in general terms, this is true of both an industrial concern and a territorial state.

In the preceding cases the development of new activities required both centralized decision-making and the use of compulsion. In some circumstances the element of compulsion may be absent, or nearly so, from a system of centralized coordination. For example, a centralized dispatching arrangement in a taxi fleet deprives the individual cab driver of the opportunity to make certain decisions on his own. It represents one form of modern centralized decision-making, though no doubt a trivial one. The dispatching system supplies the driver with fares much more continuously than is possible without this device. In this case, since centralized decision-making assists the individuals in the group to achieve their individual purposes, i.e., making money by driving taxis, there is little or no objection to the system.

If we wished to be absolutely precise in our terminology, we might call such cases examples of the concentration of authority, as distinguished from the concentration of power. Since the distinction requires knowledge about the subjective feelings of those who obey, it is far from an easy one to apply in practice. Both elements are present in widely varying proportions in any concrete case. This essay will concentrate on the type of situation in which the element of compulsion plays a major part, though the element of accepted authority will also be observed in many of them.

The second type of situation suggested as the source of power-seeking movements is one of external shock or internal decay. To choose a remote example first, the forceful unification of China for the first time, in the third century B.C., by means that recall modern totalitarian movements, was preceded by the disintegration of an earlier form of agrarian society with some resemblances to European feudalism. Communications improved, the use of iron increased, and the rigid barriers between social classes began to dissolve. The time was also one of intellectual ferment about which Mencius exclaimed bitterly, "Sage kings cease to arise . . . and unemployed scholars indulge in unreasonable discussions." [3] The essence of such situations is that human institutions fail to satisfy the expectations put upon them by a significant portion of the people living under them. A period of widespread and prolonged unemployment produces exactly these consequences in modern industrial society. Then the family breadwinner literally cannot fulfill the expectations laid upon him by his own conscience, by the members of his family, his friends, and the rest of the community.

This type of institutional failure can come about either through damage from external and internal sources to the political and social structure, or through changes in the purely subjective factor of the level of expectations itself. Poverty can exist for centuries and be regarded as part of the nature of the cosmos until a different way of looking at the world becomes available, frequently through contact with another society. The importance of this element in contemporary Asian revolutions has often been pointed out. Though the subjective factor of a change in the level of expectations can be separated from the objective elements of the economic and political structure, the two ordinarily change together.[4]

One possible consequence of institutional failure may be an added flow of power to whatever central authority already exists. Toynbee regards empire-building as the symptom and consequence of social disintegration, and has collected a number of illustrations.[5] Examining crises or institutional failures within a shorter time period, Sorokin has collected a number of cases purporting to show that political centralization is the typical response.[6]

The characteristic course of events is that the central authority finds it necessary, and often also agreeable, to substitute decisions made by itself for those made by individuals in a more diffuse manner throughout the society. Where the diffuse system of decision-making breaks down, as in the collapse of price cues for producers' decisions in a depression, the central authority substitutes its own cues and decisions. In some cases power and responsibility may be thrust upon people against their will, while in others they may be actively sought by ambitious individuals.

Not always, however, does the failure of a social system lead to a strengthening of the position of those at its apex. On more or less a priori grounds, one might suspect that the opposite course of events occurs more frequently. As the supporting institutional framework is eroded, it may collapse under the rulers instead of providing greater opportunities and demands for intervention and revolution by administrative fiat. There may be a breakup of the larger system into smaller units warring with one another, as happened repeatedly in India and China, as well as in Europe with the disintegration of the Roman Empire. Modern technology may make this particular form of disintegration unlikely in the future, though it cannot be ruled out completely.

The partial failure of a set of institutions to live up to what is expected of them provides an atmosphere receptive to demands for a more or less extensive overhaul of the status quo. At this juncture the future course of events depends heavily upon the models of a better world that become available to various strategic groups in the population. In the meantime the rulers may increase their efforts to prevent the population from gaining access to any models except those of their own creation, whose virtues they may stress with an increasingly frantic tone.

As a third very general source and type of political consolidation and expansion I have suggested the term "monarchical absolutism." It may be distinguished from the preceding one partly on the ground that it does not necessarily derive from the disintegration of a previously existing social system, though in some cases, particularly the rise of the Romanoffs, and perhaps some Asiatic despotisms, this may play an important part.

The central feature of absolute monarchy is that the ruler of one segment of a large and loosely organized polity imposes himself upon and brings order to the larger group. Purely personal factors, such as the ambition of an able and energetic ruler, may under favorable circumstances be all that is required to start the process of acquiring power in the form of monarchical absolutism. Especially in its early stages, monarchical absolutism does not appear to be propelled forward by the deep tides of economic and social change. Once the process has begun, a tradition may be established that it is the duty of the monarch to expand and consolidate his authority through incorporating various classes and interest groupings in the service of the state.[7] Since the monarch who fails to do this runs the risk of losing his authority to vigorous domestic and foreign rivals, the process perpetuates itself. It is worth noting that monarchical absolutism usually takes a long time, as much as several hundred years, to run its course.

Roughly the sequence of events just described appears to have taken place in France with the rise of the Capetian dynasty in the tenth century and the extension of the monarch's role, with occasional interruptions and retrogressions, up to the Revolution.[8] An approximately parallel growth took place in Prussia and Russia. In India the same phenomenon occurred several times, as vigorous indigenous or foreign dynasties managed to establish peace and order over a substantial part of the peninsula.

In the course of extending their power, the rulers of a developing absolutism are likely to produce their own distinctive rationalizations and doctrines, such as the divine right of kings, or the Confucian ethic of China. But, in contrast with totalitarian regimes, there remain considerable areas of social life with which the absolute monarch does not seek to interfere. In *The Age of Absolutism,* Max Beloff points out that in spite of their claims of absolute power these monarchs were "in a sense conservative, since legitimacy was of their essence." Power was limited by law and custom and compelled to respect large areas of the status quo. Existing privileges and vested interests were strong enough to resist central coordination.[9] Monarchical absolutism does not display the same intention or capacity to reconstruct the entire social order as do revolutionary movements arising out of a period of social decay.

II

All groups and individuals who seek power are discontented about some aspect of the society in which they live. In many cases the discontent merely reflects the fact that one person wants power when another person happens to have it. There is no demand for changing the structure of the system itself. For the rest of this discussion we may leave this form of personal ambition aside, with only occasional observations, in order to concentrate upon the growth patterns of movements that arise out of a failure of social institutions to match human expectations. Discontent in this setting is likely to express itself in the formulation of a doctrine.

The creation of a doctrine has often been one of the very first steps along the road the power. With widely varying degrees of elaboration, the doctrine provides an explanation of what is wrong with the current state of affairs and what should be done to correct this state. We may designate such a doctrine the charter myth of a power-seeking organization.

Probably no charter myth has ever been completely static. Instead it undergoes modification and elaboration in response to the vicissitudes of the organization's life. In this connection it is worth noticing that in the course of its growth a doctrine does not necessarily become milder and more tolerant as it becomes incorporated into a working institutional system. The Inquisition, as is well known, was a relatively late development in Christianity, organized partly to counter indiscriminate popular frenzy against those who professed unpopular opinions. In Islam one may point to the strenuous efforts of the seventeenth-century Mogul emperor Aurangzeb to uproot and destroy Hinduism, after an extended period of religious tolerance by his predecessors.[10] The emergence of a real or imaginary threat to rulers whose power has a strong theocratic tinge may bring about a compulsory orthodoxy which is more repressive than that found in the early and fanatical stages of a movement, because it has more powerful instruments at its command.

Any concrete charter myth, such as Christianity or Marxism, contains a mixture of truth and propaganda. A large portion of political theory concerns itself with the critical evaluation of such myths from a variety of ethical positions. No such attempt can be made here, and the discussion will be confined to a few empirical suggestions concerning the content and structure of such myths.

Among the enormous variety of charter myths that have arisen in the course of human history, one may distinguish two frequently recurring issues. One issue is that of nativism versus xenophilia. By nativism I mean an energetic and somewhat distorted reaffirmation of the indigenous way of life, a reaction often produced in a society that feels itself threatened by forces beyond its understanding and control. But social disturbances may also produce xenophilia, or a longing to copy the ways of another culture. The other issue is that of hierarchy and discipline versus equality and freedom. A "time of troubles" may produce demands for either more or less equality, often in terms of some larger principle such as race or reason. Either hierarchy or equality may conceivably be combined with one of the remaining pair, nativism or xenophilia.

The combination of nativism with a stress on discipline and authority yields a result familiar in the modern world, called pseudo-conservatism in its more diffuse social manifestations, and fascism when it becomes an organized political movement.[11] The partial breakup of a society can result in a call for a return to some semi-imaginary past, and a reaffirmation of the sturdier virtues, in order to attain a hoped-for future. This result is, perhaps, especially likely to occur where the virtues of physical courage, self-control, and subordination to authority have been successful in the past. In its early stages, the pseudo-conservative movement can take the form of support for the existing rulers. In any case, those in power are likely to try to make use of it. The erosion of the status quo may produce a Cato before it brings forth a Catiline or a Hitler. Pseudo-conservatism, however, soon goes beyond the status quo to demand a thorough redistribution of privilege and authority. As in the Nazi movement, or even in extreme right-wing Republican statements in the United States, pseudo-conservatism calls for the overthrow of the existing regime on the grounds that it has grown "too soft" or has made its way to power through "treachery" to the ancient way of life.

Where nativism and egalitarianism are combined in a charter myth, the egalitarian aspect often falls short of universal application. Sparta, living under the permanent emergency of a Helot revolt, constitutes a well-known example. There the equality prevailing in the ruling caste did not of course extend to the suppressed Helots. In nationalist movements, too, the conception of equality is ambiguous. During the early stages, admiration for the oppressor may occur along with a demand for equality with the dominant group. Both themes are very noticeable in Indian nationalism. Even the Nazis displayed some Anglophile sentiments, particularly admiration for the supposed cunning of the British aristocracy, regarded as the major reason for the German defeat in 1918. Later such admiration may turn to hate. One might summarize the characteristic stages of development in a series of slogans. First: "We ought to be equal to you, our oppressors!" Second: "We really are equal to you, our oppressors!" Third: "We are superior to you and everyone else, though in comparison to such unfortunates as you, we are equal among ourselves!" Thus for nativist movements the doctrine of equality serves two purposes. It furnishes the ground for denying the out-group's claim of superiority. And it emphasizes similarities within the in-group, in order to distinguish the in-group from the out-group.

Nativism represents a twisted or idealized affirmation of the existing order, so twisted as to be genuinely revolutionary. Nevertheless, in its more developed form of a fanatical religious or secular patriotism, nativism is always tied to a particular group. In Germany it may take the form of National Socialism, while in Japan it appears in the guise of a revival of the imperial cult. In India it becomes Hindu or Islamic communalism, and in the United States 200 per cent Americanism.

Egalitarianism, on the other hand, generally represents a rejection and negation of the existing order. This fact may account for what appears to be its greater capacity for xenophilia. English egalitarianism once looked to the French Revolution, while the French revolutionists looked to republican Rome, the Greek tyrannicides, or to an imaginary state of nature. About equalitarian movements among American Negroes it has often been observed that their center of gravity lies outside the Negro caste, and that they take their standards of behavior from the American middle class.

In contrast to nativism, egalitarianism represents a universal, though utopian, principle for the ordering of social relationships. For this reason its appeal can readily transcend national and religious boundaries. During the initial stages of political upheaval, this universal quality may constitute one of the strategic advantages of Communism over nativist forms of authoritarian rule, especially in Asia. However, as the superpatriotism of latter-day Stalinism demonstrates, once an egalitarian revolution acquires a territorial base and a vested interest in a particular social order, it may acquire the traits we have noticed in nativism.

As a program in its own right, egalitarianism by definition calls for the replacement of the status quo by a society in which the prevailing inequalities will be leveled out or perhaps merely reversed. It may take either a secular or a religious form, an attempt at the active reconstruction of the world or a withdrawal from it. Even in the latter instance, as in monasticism in both its Asiatic and Western forms, it may achieve considerable secular power. However, since the acquisition of power requires the development of hierarchy and discipline at some point, an egalitarian movement starts off at an initial disadvantage in relation to its competitors. Sooner or later, if it is to be effective, it must compromise with its initial principles. Christianity required several centuries to reach this compromise, while Marxism, especially in its Leninist version, reached this stage very rapidly.[12]

Thus the quest for power is justified in terms of some larger scheme of values. For the early stages of a movement, therefore, it is probably always correct to assert that power is an instrumental value, something that is sought not in its own right, but to obtain something else. Very rapidly, however, power tends to become an ultimate value. The very fact that power is such a vital instrument in the pursuit of many other values tends to transform it, in the course of its acquisition, from a mere instrument to an end in itself. The process may be clearly observed in the rise of the Papacy and in Russian Marxism, as well as in many other movements.

In addition to providing a justification for the search for power, the charter myth usually contains at least rudimentary rules for the allocation of authority within the power-seekers' own organization. As part of such rules there is also some explicit or implicit provision designating what persons may interpret the doctrine in the future. Still another very significant aspect of the charter myth is the definition of membership in the group.

Among these rules, the one defining membership may be the most important in giving the group its character. A sharp boundary line between those who belong and those who do not aids a movement in preserving its identity in the course of subsequent struggles. The necessity to preserve this boundary line becomes increasingly important the more a movement seeks to control the entire span of the individual member's behavior, personality, and inmost thoughts. Thus the early Christian communities were at first "bound together merely by the ties of spontaneous aggregation," though they could refuse membership to persons deemed unworthy of it. At an early period the test of membership became the act of partaking of the Lord's Supper. Out of this early symbolism there grew the dread power of excommunication.[13] Certain aspects of the definition of membership in the Christian community, particularly the treatment of those whose faith had temporarily lapsed under the stress of persecution, became a matter of acrid dispute among the early bishops.[14] In general, the struggle over doctrine and personnel may easily lead to serious splits in the early stages of a movement. This has been true not only of groups that begin with a rejection of the pursuit of secular power, such as Christianity and Buddhism, but also of movements with stronger political emphasis, such as Islam and of course Marxism.

In the course of such struggles, a marked strategic advantage accrues to the victorious faction if it can also establish that no rules governing the appointment of people to various posts and no element in the doctrine are immune to interpretation by whatever person stands at the apex of the organization.[15] The struggle of the Roman bishops to gain exclusive authority over doctrine and the appointment of subordinates constitutes the major theme of early church history. During these internal conflicts, the popes made use of forgeries that in scope and boldness of execution far surpass the Stalinist rewriting of history for similar purposes.[16]

Thus the main function of the charter myth lies in the establishment of legitimacy, or obedience that will occur without coercion. Through rules governing the allocation of authority within a power-seeking organization, it provides the basis of legitimacy within such a group. Through its public program and the doctrines used to justify this program, it attempts to establish a similar basis for obedience and acceptance within the larger society.

III

Now we may examine some of the alternatives facing the seekers after power in their subsequent efforts to master the internal environment of their own organization and the external environment of the larger society.[17] We may begin with the conception of a small group of men known personally to one another. It may be the ruler and his associates who have limited authority over a small area and wish to extend this authority much more widely. Or it may be a group that is out of power in a particular state or community. (In the latter case, the members of the group will probably be united around some program, which need not have secular power as its objective.) Such a group may be regarded as the primary cell, with the leader as its nucleus, out of which a larger and more differentiated social structure may grow.

One process that may occur, especially if the original nucleus is not committed to the pursuit of secular power, is growth by simple division and the formation of new cells. This is roughly what happened in the spread of the Christian communities around the Mediterranean basin in the first centuries of our era. However, if the group takes up the pursuit of secular power, simple cell division will probably turn out to be no more than a beginning stage and a transition to other more tightly knit and hierarchical structures. Indeed, because the early Christian communities were larger than the original body of apostles, they adopted a more hierarchical arrangement for settling their internal affairs. In turn, this hierarchical arrangement set the pattern for the efforts of one of the divisions, the Roman see, to take command of the entire Christian world.[18]

One way in which a hierarchical structure may emerge is through the extension of the personal relationships and personal loyalties that exist within the original nucleus to a wider circle of people. This process results in the spread of a diffuse obligation, covering a wide variety of activities. The outcome may be provisionally labeled "feudalism," a form that has arisen in may parts of the world. As is well known, feudalism may also grow from the bottom upward as inferiors commit themselves to superiors for protection. Repeated experience in both Europe and Asia demonstrates that feudal relationships are adequate to coordinate, at least loosely, the activities of a large number of people over a wide area of territory.

Though feudalism constitutes a much more distinctly hierarchical form of coordination and growth than cell division, it remains a very loose form of social organization. It will not serve to focus the energies and activities of a large number of people on a narrow social front or upon a single goal. Under feudalism the leader turns over to his subordinate a piece of territory to do with as he likes provided certain minimal obligations of loyalty, military support, or tribute are met. In the same way, the inferior may commit himself to the charge of a superior in return for protection. The relationship that arises is a personal one that includes within it a large variety of functions and obligations. Its diffuse nature makes it an inadequate instrument for a vigorous group with a definite policy in mind which the group wishes to impose on an extensive territory or a large number of people.[19]

A rational bureaucracy, with its firm allocation of rights and duties for each post in a well-defined chain of command, is a far superior instrument for the execution of a definite policy. In its classic form, made familiar through Weber's analysis, a bureaucracy controls very specifically a limited range of the activities of the subordinate members. One gives and receives orders only in one's official capacity. In a large corporation the vice-president in charge of sales can require his subordinates to drop one kind of selling technique and adopt another. But he cannot impose a *corvée* or the requirement of military service on the company salesmen. Their obligation is limited to selling the company products. Furthermore, the company is free to discharge inadequate salesmen and hire better ones, while the salesman becomes an interchangeable part, able to perform as effectively for one company as another — if he is lucky enough to get a job.

Under feudalism the system of interchangeable parts does not exist, or occurs on a very restricted scale. The serf is tied to the land and the vassal to his overlord. But feudal relationships may be transformed into bureaucratic ones in a variety of ways. An increase in the number of activities carried on within a society brings with it the specialization that modifies the diffuse feudal bond. An attempt to impose more precise coordination and greater economic burdens for military purposes has similar consequences. Both elements were significant in the rise of royal absolutism in Europe.

The transformation required the destruction of the old order, sometimes peacefully and gradually but more often violently and painfully, as part of the birth pangs of the new.

Just as feudalism may be transformed into rationalist bureaucracy through the effort to achieve a closer control over the activities of a group, so may the rationalist and legal bureaucracy be transformed into a totalitarian hierarchical structure. From the standpoint of the supreme authority, the chief defect of a bureaucracy is that it operates according to rules that are impersonal and not subject to ready change. These rules, necessary to give a bureaucracy its qualities of regularity and precision, also serve to inhibit the leader from exercising his power fully.

In the absence of rules, on the other hand, the supreme authority in a totalitarian system can alter policy and shift the personal instruments of his power with minimal hindrance from the organization. In this manner he can nip attachments to a particular locality or to a particular function, such as the military, economic, police, or propaganda, before they can consolidate themselves and become a threat. For this reason a totalitarian ruler makes strong efforts to be informed about every local quarrel and to act as the authority that settles these quarrels. At the same time he frequently jumps over intervening links in the chain of command to make his power felt at the lowest levels.[20] What I have elsewhere called the "vested interest in confusion" seems to be an essential element in the internal dynamics of totalitarianism.

Also in contrast to rational bureaucracy, totalitarian rule seeks a full commitment of the subordinate's personality to the dictator's objectives. In this way it represents an extension of the charismatic relationship that binds the original band of followers to the leader. Just as they are to devote their whole lives and feelings to the leader's mission, so also are the subsequent adherents. Naturally this commitment is never fully realized in practice. It rapidly becomes diluted, as the movement grows, and is replaced by other bonds, such as the bureaucratic and the feudal types. Nevertheless, the movement may retain, and even elaborate, some traits designed to prevent the followers from developing strong external attachments that would divert resources and energies away from the group goal. The practice of sacerdotal celibacy is a well-known example. It appears to have been demanded, in the Catholic Church, mainly to prevent the clergy from acquiring property interests in conflict with the Roman hierarchy.[21] Personal relationships with those outside the movement or hostile to it may be forbidden, as is the case with Communists. The round of internal activities and rituals may be increased so as to absorb the whole of the member's time and energy.

If we leave aside the simple process of cell division, the internal aspects of the growth of a power structure out of a single cell consist essentially in the allocation of human and material resources to subordinates, along with a corresponding allocation of tasks or functions, combined with devices to ensure loyalty and obedience to the guiding nucleus. Among such devices coercion plays a well-known role. Where the allocation of resources is emphasized, subsequent development takes the form of feudalism or tax farming. Where the allocation of functions is stressed, rational bureaucracy arises. Totalitarianism represents, in part, an attempt to allocate functions without granting control over the resources that the function requires, in order to prevent the growth of independent bases of power in the hands of subordinates.

To avoid possible misunderstanding, it is perhaps necessary to point out that there is no inevitable sequence of stages in the forms of feudalism, rational bureaucracy, and totalitarian hierarchy. Each of the three, as I have tried to indicate, contains within it disruptive forces that can transform it into either of the other two.[22] But it would be a mistake to regard these tendencies as merely disruptive. It is highly likely that none of the three types of hierarchical structure sketched in the last few paragraphs could ever exist in a pure form. Even the most cold-blooded and precision-minded rational bureaucracy expends considerable effort to build up organizational loyalty. It also demands certain standards of behavior outside the office as well as during working hours, often on pain of dismissal. In other words, it displays certain feudal and totalitarian traits. Likewise, no feudal system will work unless a superior can give at least some orders and expect them to be carried out in the manner of a rational bureaucracy. The same is true of a totalitarian dictator. Since no one system will operate successfully by itself, traits must be adopted from the others to supplement its internal deficiencies. In turn, the adoption of these traits may undermine the system. Any concrete and empirical system of power and authority is likely to contain an unstable mixture of the three. The situation recalls the

Hegelian dialectic with emphasis on inevitable internal contradictions.[23]

As we turn from the internal aspects of growth to the external ones, i.e., the relationships between the power-seeking group and the surrounding society, it is possible to distinguish at least four recurring problems that are faced by any group as it tries to establish legitimacy and control in the larger arena. One problem is that of finding or constructing a body of supporters. Such a clientele may range from a small tightly knit body to a large and amorphous mass following. Another and closely related problem concerns the kinds of tactical alliances, if any, that are sought in the struggle for political victory. Some groups display a marked willingness to enter into tactical alliances at considerable cost to their program and organizational identity, while others try to maintain a position of splendid isolation and doctrinal purity. The third and fourth problems occur only when and if power is achieved. Then there is the problem either of sharing it, as in the form of a coalition or the toleration of organized opposition, or of rejecting political partnership. Finally, there is the choice between leaving the existing structure unchanged — as happens, for example, after a palace revolution — or using power to alter or pulverize the old structures, such as social classes and estates, religious bodies, economic corporations, guilds, trade unions, and even kinship structures and the family — all in order to create a new structure.

The way in which these problems are solved depends not only upon the structure of the group that seeks power, but also upon the structure of the society in which the search takes place. In some cases, the disturbance spreads to neighboring societies, and they too become part of the relevant environment of those who pursue power. Here the discussion will be limited to a few concluding observations on the influence of structural differences in the surrounding society upon these four choices.

Let us consider first a stable society, in which most of the population accepts most features of the status quo, and where authority is sufficiently diffused so that there is no readily identifiable and single set of levers of command sufficiently powerful to set the whole society in motion in a given direction. Around the turn of the century, after the first wave of industrialism had passed over it, American society still approximated this model. Then Bryce could write of American public opinion that political light and heat radiated from no single center. Instead, our basic consensus arose primarily out of myriad individual interchanges.[24]

Where these conditions prevail, a group that seeks a substantial share in power must be able to combine a large variety of minor contradictions to create a broad political base. This is the familiar pattern of a democratic political party. A group that has a wide range of severe grievances against the status quo and is organized around a comprehensive program cannot mobilize sufficient support to gain overwhelming power. Instead, there tends to be a large number of pressure groups with individual grievances. These do their best to reward their friends and punish their enemies. But they display little interest in gaining control of the society as a whole. The power-seekers in such a society are pushed toward the choice of creating a large clientele and of making numerous loose tactical alliances. When formally in power, they must share it through the toleration of organized opposition and confine themselves to moderately reformist programs meeting immediate grievances.

In a stable despotism, too, most of the people accept most features of the status quo. The various empires in India at the apogee of their power may serve as a satisfactory empirical example. Such a situation provides the most favorable background for a palace revolution. Under these conditions, a group that tries to carry out a coup does not require any mass clientele or any tactical alliances that spread deep into the society. All that is necessary is the benevolent neutrality of key elements among the higher élite, particularly the group that controls the instruments of violence. The new rulers can grasp the levers of command, after which life proceeds much as it did before. Instability at the top may not seriously damage the rest of the society for a long time, as the four centuries of the Roman Empire suggest. In such instances, then, the solution of these problems takes the form of minimal clientele and tactical alliances, and the monopoly of power by those who seize it. The rulers must of course be certain of at least the passive acceptance of their supremacy by the key elements in the society — the priesthood, the military, and the heads of major economic units. Should totalitarianism stabilize itself in the course of the twentieth century and lose the *élan* with which it rose to power, this ancient political pattern might reassert itself.

The transformation and decay of a society call for still other solutions. In the modern world, the sources of this

transformation may be found partly in the structural difficulties inherent in modern industrialism, some of which
were foreseen by Marxists around the turn of the century,[25]
and partly in the erosion of traditional values and beliefs by
modern secular rationalism. As Western industrialism and
rationalism have spread eastward, into Russia and the
Orient, they have speeded the decay of ancient social systems.
As already noted, such periods of rapid change favor the
rise of either nativist or egalitarian movements with comprehensive philosophies — or pseudo-philosophies, as they
are termed by their opponents. Such movements are likely
to develop totalitarian features.

A totalitarian movement tries to acquire a considerable
mass clientele, especially from individuals turned loose upon
the world by the destruction of prior social bonds. It is, on
the other hand, chary of tactical alliances. It may enter into
alliances, but where it does so, it seeks to dominate its partners, or else to isolate and destroy them one by one. The
notion of mutual gains through mutual compromises is
foreign to fanatical movements, though in time such behavior may be forced upon them by the sheer requirements
of survival. Soon after it gains power, though not necessarily immediately afterward, the totalitarian movement
does its best to pulverize and atomize those segments of
society that have maintained some degree of corporate
identity. Others it seeks to control by penetration both before
and after the seizure of power. In so doing a totalitarian
regime is aided by the process of atomization and the
destruction of the traditional order that precedes its rise to
power. Along with these destructive processes, a totalitarian

movement seeks to create new institutions and new levers of command that will give it something approaching its ultimate goal of total control of all social activities.

IV

The preceding pages are not and do not purport to be a complete theory of power, even in sketchy outline form. They have stressed the acquisition of power and mentioned the growth of checks on power-holders only incidentally. Any adequate theory of power would have to take as much account of the latter as the former, as well as of many other elements that I have altogether failed to discuss. Yet, by way of conclusion, the suggestion may be offered that there are at least four discernible processes of acquiring power that take their essential pattern from the way in which the process begins. The totalitarian one, in either its nativist or egalitarian forms, is perhaps the easiest to recognize. Its source lies in shock to a social system or the more gradual decay of existing institutions, and the rise of new demands on these institutions. Its charter myth soon develops a stress on hierarchy. Subsequently it develops its own characteristic internal structure and way of coping with the external social environment. Monarchical absolutism, the second pattern, may begin under conditions of greater fragmentation than totalitarianism. It advances more slowly and is perhaps more the consequence of individual ambition than deeper social causes. Despite some of the pretensions of its charter myth, it is strongly conservative and unable to free itself from dependence on strongly established vested interests.

Though its internal structure may contain some elements prominent in totalitarianism, such as espionage within its hierarchical instruments, the element of rational bureaucracy, with its allocation of rights and duties to specific stations according to universal norms, is perhaps more important. Reluctant to share power with other groups in the society, it must necessarily do so. As a third pattern, the rise of new activities, for which I will refrain from coining any special term, can be expected to produce a charter myth with a strong emphasis on hierarchy if these activities are ones that go counter to long-established human wants. If, on the contrary, these activities are ones that a substantial number of people wish to pursue, the charter myth may take an egalitarian form or even deny the relevance of authority. For example, early industrialism in England was accompanied by the development of classical economic theory with its stress on the "invisible hand." Finally, feudalism appears to be a transition form that may emerge out of the decay of a more centralized regime or, perhaps less frequently, out of a highly fragmented polity that has never known centralization. Its charter myth places a high emphasis on loyalty to a person instead of to an office, which in turn limits the forms of subsequent growth.

Though each of these four types may go through its own distinctive process of growth and decay, there does not seem to be any inevitable sequence of stages in which one type, such as monarchical absolutism or feudalism, necessarily precedes or follows other types. The forms distinguished here appear to be recurring subpatterns within the over-all process of irreversible historical development that characterizes human society as a whole. None of them occurs in an absolutely pure form. Instead significant variations are found in these subpatterns at each stage of human history. For example, in the pre-industrial world the basic features of centralized totalitarian regimes have emerged in several countries, as pointed out in the next essay, while on the other hand the rise of modern industry has introduced significant new elements into the totalitarian complex. To trace the historical fate of each of these four types would be an enormous task far beyond the limits of this essay. If these tentative formulations are near the mark, one would expect to find during any given historical epoch an emphasis upon one of these forms combined with a subordinate utilization of the others.

· 2 ·

TOTALITARIAN ELEMENTS
IN PRE-INDUSTRIAL SOCIETIES

Ueberall im Studium mag man mit den
Anfängen beginnen, nur bei der Geschichte nicht.

Burckhardt

Both the conservative and the radical critiques of modern
society converge on one major thesis. They explain the rise
of totalitarian regimes and of a totalitarian atmosphere in
formally democratic countries as the consequence of certain
processes at work in industrial society. I believe that this
indictment contains much that is sound and hope some day
to complete an extensive examination of it. Here I propose
to undertake little more than a preliminary reconnaissance
by examining totalitarian or quasi-totalitarian practices in
pre-industrial societies. Through such an examination one
may hope to discover those aspects of modern times that
have their analogues in earlier days and therefore cannot
be attributed wholly to industrialism. In this way it may be
possible to clear the ground of certain misconceptions.

Before proceeding further it may be worthwhile to spend
a moment clarifying what we mean by the word totalitarian.
The discussion will be brief because I do not believe that we
can define a subject until we know what we are talking
about, and we cannot know what we are talking about until

we have examined it thoroughly. Clear ideas are the results of scientific inquiry rather than its preliminary tools. Nevertheless it is only fair to the reader to spare him from following the investigator into all the brambly bypaths where the research has led, and to indicate in advance the main directions of an inquiry.

First of all, the term totalitarian as used in this essay implies coercion or repression. Since nearly all human societies, excepting perhaps a few of the simplest nonliterate ones, contain substantial elements of coercion, this first approximation does not get us very far. We mean more than that. As the root "total" suggests, writers who use this term usually have in mind a society all of whose activities, from the rearing of children to the production and distribution of economic goods, are controlled and directed from a single center. Presumably coercion plays a large part in this centralized control. No known society of course has ever coincided exactly with this conception. The concept merely denotes a limit to which various societies may approach. With this scheme in mind, it would then be possible to arrange any number of actual societies in a series according to the degree to which they approached this limit. Although there would be difficulties in obtaining the necessary facts and in interpreting them correctly, in principle the problem is soluble and provides a definite meaning for the term totalitarian. This concept of centralized totalitarianism is the one that coincides most closely with general scholarly usage.[1] In history the various political systems that approach a centralized form of totalitarianism are the common ones.

But centralized totalitarianism is not necessarily the only

possible species in the general class of repressive societies. In the course of reflecting on the cases examined and discussing with other scholars their resemblances to and differences from modern centralized totalitarianism, I gradually became aware that a decentralized and diffuse system of repression willingly accepted by the mass of the population constitutes another very important possibility. Such attitudes of course exist also among the people in modern states of the centralized variety, particularly in the earliest stages of enthusiasm, but they are not enough to make the system run by itself. Under a system of decentralized or "popular" totalitarianism the authority of a central government would exert less control than spontaneous mutual repression. In the extreme or limiting case it might be possible to dispense with centrally organized repression. Though very small hints of the potential role of mutual repression occur in a few pre-industrial societies, it is the advance of modern industrialism that may create for the first time conditions favorable for its realization on a substantial scale. Industrialism can make centralized totalitarianism vastly more efficient and terrible than anything that has gone before. Nevertheless some future historian might decide that the more important consequence was the emergence of "popular" totalitarianism. This possibility can be discussed more realistically and effectively after examining the more traditional versions of totalitarianism.

Any investigation such as this one is liable to certain limitations and possible misunderstandings which it will be wise to recognize at the outset. In the first place, as Professor Herbert Marcuse has pointed out, we cannot justify contemporary repression merely by asserting that similar practices have existed in the past. They may not be necessary now, under the new conditions provided by technological advance.[2] Slavery may have been a necessary institution to get society's work done in past ages. In a machine civilization there may no longer be any justification for it. At the same time, to return to our central problem, it would be an obvious logical error to attribute all the slavish aspects of modern society wholly to industrialism when we know about their existence in previous epochs. What we want to find out eventually, then, is the extent to which modern industrial society has produced new forms of repression, if any, and modified old ones.

In the second place, it is misleading merely to search the record of history for more or less adequate parallels to twentieth-century totalitarianism. History, for reasons set down elsewhere, cannot be treated as a grab bag from which a researcher draws forth statistical samples of certain kinds of behavior.[3] Adequate understanding requires that both early and modern forms of despotism be correctly placed in a general context of the growth of human institutions and therefore requires as much knowledge of the differences between early and modern despotism as it does of their similarities.

For these reasons, as well as more human limitations, I have not attempted to draw from history a "representative" sample of despotic regimes or quasi-totalitarian practices. Two thoughts have governed the selection of the cases treated here. First of all, I have chosen examples that on preliminary inspection seemed to show readily recognizable similarities to the ideas and practices of modern totalitarian regimes, particularly Stalinist Russia and National Socialist Germany. In the second place, since most previous attempts along these lines have drawn exclusively on European experience,[4] I have tried to widen our intellectual horizon in both time and space, through the discussion of certain practices in nonliterate societies and an analysis of China and India during what historians tell us are the most despotic periods in their history. To these cases I have added that of Geneva under Calvin, as a specimen halfway between Oriental despotism and twentieth-century totalitarianism. Like many medieval eschatological movements, Calvinist Geneva also shows signs of an early stage of "popular" totalitarianism in its emphasis on "equality" and lip service to democratic practices. In studying these cases I was necessarily limited to the use of source materials in European languages, some of which were translations of original documents on China, India, and Geneva. One can only hope that the illumination which comes from a broader comparative standpoint may compensate for the loss that comes from the lack of firsthand familiarity with the sources.

II

On first consideration, nonliterate societies would seem an unpromising place to search for analogues to modern totalitarianism. In such societies, the basic cells of human society — kinship units, and small territorial units such as the village — constitute the structure within which the life of the society ebbs and flows. As a rule, the power and authority of what we, using the terminology of our own culture, would call a political leader is substantially less in nonliterate societies than in those with a written language, where the state generally prevails.[5]

There are some exceptions, and it will be worthwhile to spend a few moments on them. Occasionally, a chieftain may win despotic power in a tribe and engage in massive acts of cruelty that recall modern totalitarian methods. About Shaka, chief of the warrior Zulus, it is said that almost every day men were summarily seized and killed on his orders, frequently in response to a mere whim. On the death of his mother, in a wild outburst of grief, he ordered the execution of several men on the spot. Then the Zulu multitudes began a general massacre of those they thought were not showing sufficient grief.[6] This episode does reveal some of the darker possibilities of human nature. It differs, however, from modern totalitarianism, in that this outburst of cruelty, even if on a mass scale and triggered by the actions of a despot, does not appear to have been part of any over-all political objective. Cruelty here seems to have come mainly from outbursts of rage instead of being primarily a deliberately chosen instrument of policy. Even the cruelty of the Mongols under Genghis Khan, a people on the borderline between literate and nonliterate society,[7] does not appear to have been a deliberate policy. Rather the nomadic warlike Mongols at first did not know what to do with civilized cities after conquering them, except to burn and pillage and to kill the inhabitants. Later, generalized terror may have been a useful device to make enemies submit.[8]

The Inca Empire of Peru is also frequently referred to as

a nonliterate precursor of modern socialist totalitarianism. I believe this interpretation is mistaken. Inca society did reach a degree of political centralization remarkable for a people without a written language. But on closer examination the aura of similarity to contemporary political systems disappears. The government neither owned nor operated the major economic undertakings. A certain proportion of fields were set aside to be cultivated by the village community for the purpose of providing tribute. Village lands were redistributed periodically, as in the Russian *mir*.[9] Such arrangements are widespread in agrarian societies and have nothing to do with modern leftist totalitarian regimes. Nor did the Inca government make much of an effort to control the daily life of the people. One authority who devoted special attention to the amount of government interference in economic, family, and religious life concluded that the Inca regime was very far from an absolutist despotism.[10]

Thus, even the most highly selective approach to the world of nonliterate societies yields very little in the way of strictly political practices that show any striking resemblance to modern totalitarianism. On the other hand, totalitarianism, as suggested above, is not necessarily limited to political centralization and might even conceivably exist without it. It is also marked by a more diffuse conformity to repressive and irrational standards of social behavior. Through an atmosphere of fear and suspicion, one sector of society is able to manipulate individual fears and aggressions to its own advantage. As soon as this aspect of totalitarianism enters our focus of attention, more similarities to it in nonliterate societies become visible. Probably the most important of these is witchcraft.

Though generalizations are of course hazardous, witchcraft in nonliterate societies is often traceable to a definite combination of circumstances. Part of the combination is a disaster, such as disease, or a more prolonged stress, such as the failure of traditional food-getting methods, for which the native culture lacks any adequate technique that would enable it to cope with the situation. Because the culture lacks this technique, groups or individuals may develop a highly personalized explanation of the disaster, that is, one couched in terms of the evil acts of particular individuals or groups of people. In turn this explanation legitimizes aggression against members of the same society. The reservoir of such "internal" aggression is probably substantial in most societies anyway, and is likely to be increased, in time at any rate, through the frustrations of want or disaster.

A few cases will help to illustrate these relationships and make them more concrete. Among the Zuni, epidemics of smallpox and measles were ascribed to witchcraft. In one of these the witch was hung up by the thumbs, the Zuni method of executing a witch, and saved only by the actions of an American school teacher.[11] Among the Bantu, there is a ceremony known as the "smelling out of the sorcerer." As soon as he is detected, even his best friends shy away from him. He is seized and tortured by fearful means to confess his guilt and reveal the magical means he used. Finally his whole property is confiscated. Since the witch process forms an easy way for the chief to enrich himself, it is the prosperous who have aroused the hostility of the chief who are especially menaced. Often it is a matter of common knowledge just who is to be smelled out.[12] In many cases, it is the foreigner or marginal member of a society, especially if he belongs to a despised group, who is liable to suspicion as a sorcerer.[13]

In a most illuminating study of witchcraft among the Navaho, Professor Clyde Kluckhohn traces the tendency to seek a personalized explanation of misfortune to a universal condition of early infancy. During that time nearly everything that happens to a child is the consequence of human acts, those of parents or their substitutes.[14] Navaho witchcraft stems from diffuse anxieties and hostilities, largely created by a deteriorating economic situation, in turn due to encroachment by the whites. Some of this hostility may be drained off by gossiping about imaginary witches or "real" ones who live in a distant place. Presumably the gratifications obtained in this way are somewhat dilute. Occasionally, however, a Navaho can get the satisfaction of actually seeing the accused suffer.

In the security of a crowd who are of one mind one can assail the witch face to face. Still more rarely, the luxury of socially sanctioned physical aggression toward an in-grouper is permitted. The fact that the killing of witches is uniformly described as violently sadistic suggests that these acts gained huge increments of displaced aggression.[15]

The combination of circumstances behind nonliterate witchcraft is also common enough in the twentieth century and leads to similar results. Modern society too confronts situations for which its culture provides no adequate solution and that lead to personalized explanations justifying aggression. The Nazi persecution of the Jews, the Stalinist purges, and, at a milder level, the McCarthy period in America, are familiar and recent examples of this ugly configuration. Only the most incurable optimist could claim that with the advance of civilization man has become progressively more able to cope rationally with his problems and thereby banish the demons of his own creation. The day may eventually come when knowledge and intelligence are a step ahead of human problems. So far the record provides little ground for complacent hope. The changes that appear as one moves from nonliterate to "advanced" civilizations are scarcely to the credit of the latter. For the most part, nonliterate religions are too hospitable to each other's deities and practices to permit the rigid and self-righteous intolerance we find in the civilizations of Europe and Asia. With the march of civilization the original elements of witchcraft remain, but take on new forms. Under a more advanced economy religious beliefs become entwined with powerful economic and political interests. Bureaucratic and more efficient devices to secure conformity arise. Thus there is nothing in nonliterate society, we are told, to correspond to the Inquisition or the witch burnings of the Middle Ages.[16] To my knowledge there is also nothing that corresponds, even making due allowance for changes of scale and proportion, to concentration camps and gas chambers. These products of "civilization" represent one of the qualitative leaps of human "progress."

III

As we turn from nonliterate societies to classic examples of ancient Oriental despotism in China and India, more distinct similarities to centralized totalitarianism emerge into view.

Nearly three thousand years ago Chinese civilization, already highly developed but still organized into relatively small conflicting units, began to move toward a social and intellectual crisis similar to that in European civilization since the decay of Christian feudalism and the rise of powerful secular states. Unlike the European case so far, however, the transformation of Chinese society culminated in the establishment of a single powerful state and the imposition of a high degree of political, linguistic, and cultural uniformity. The process was largely completed under the Ch'in dynasty (221–209 B.C.), from which comes the name China. Though the dynasty itself was short-lived, and is synonymous with terror and tyranny in Chinese historiography, Western historians tell us that the pattern of institutions which crystallized under the Ch'in influenced very heavily the practice of government under subsequent powerful emperors.[17] Quite possibly important traces of this influence remain even in Communist China.

Our knowledge of the structure of Chinese society prior to its temporary unification under the Ch'in is uncertain. Some scholars see in the relationships between lord and peasant of that period a situation that justifies the designation feudal. Others shy away from the term. The reasons for the decay of the older system are also subjects of an acrimonious debate among the specialists. One theory, put forward by Wolfram Eberhard, accepts the designation feudalism for this early period, and explains it as the result of the conquest of a basically agrarian group by a nomadic one. In turn the rise of a money economy, he tells us, played an important part in the disintegration of the earlier society and its transformation into despotism.[18] Sharply critical of this interpretation is Karl Wittfogel, who has adopted and extended the suggestions of Marx and Weber in maintaining that irrigation and flood control systems managed by the central government lie at the root of Oriental despotism.[19] A well-known French historian advances still another interpretation. He claims that the invention of a plough that could be drawn by animal power, toward the middle of the fifth century B.C., was fatal to the solidary bonds that had previously united lord and peasant. Gradually, permanent fields took the place of periodic clearings and thereby produced changes in territory, social organization, and religion.[20] At that time too iron was coming into general use, communications improving, and the rigid division between social classes disappearing.[21] Whatever the exact situation may have been, a question that must be left to the specialists, the fact of an important social and economic revolution culminating in despotism is undeniable.

It is also reasonably clear that the decay of the older society facilitated the establishment of despotism through the destruction of older social structures. The process recalls certain discussions of modern mass society where the individual also is supposedly left exposed as the advance of industrialism erodes the older bonds of family, social class, profession, and others, to create an amorphous mass of individuals easily subject to manipulation by demagogues.[22]

In the early history of China the process ran about as follows. Before the establishment of major changes in the fourth to third centuries B.C., Chinese agriculture was apparently based on a system of rotating the fields brought under cultivation. The patriarchal family constituted the central cell in this arrangement, known as the *ching t'ien* or "well-field" system. In some areas at any rate, though not in all, land was divided into squares, while each square was further subdivided into nine smaller units, thus:

Eight families cultivated the plots on the sides, while the central plot was cultivated in common to raise produce for taxes. After the land was exhausted, the peasants moved on to another area. Though we cannot be sure about the extent to which this schematic description is colored by the idealization of Chinese writers who looked back to an earlier Golden Age, some modern authorities accept it as a rough approximation of the major institutional arrangements prior to the rise of the Ch'in.[23] In any case Chinese historical tradition preserves the memory of a society preceding the Ch'in that was very different from what came to pass.

With the advance of settled agriculture the earlier system probably tended to disintegrate of its own accord. Therefore we cannot accept at face value the statement by Chinese historians that Lord Shang (Wei Yang), a famous adviser of the duke of Ch'in in the fourth century B.C., abolished the *ching t'ien* system and replaced it with a system of more permanent private property in land.[24] Almost certainly the changes were part of a much longer development.

On the other hand, there are strong indications of the way the ruler tried to take advantage of this process. Lord Shang is said to have reorganized the people into groups of fives and tens to control one another and to share one another's punishments. They were also obliged to denounce each other's crimes.[25] Thus the partial breakup of the older family and landholding institutions enabled the ruler to take advantage of individual antagonisms and suspicions in much the same way as occurs in modern totalitarian states.

As part of the same transition we find the rapid growth of a centrally controlled bureaucracy. Where formerly the farmers' taxes had probably gone to the local lord, they were now levied by officials and sent to the granaries of the capital.[26] In 350 B.C. Lord Shang had carried out a territorial reform, organizing the small cities and towns in the state of Ch'in into a total of thirty-one *hsien,* each under the administration of a prefect.[27] Through this bureaucracy a degree of standardization and uniformity, which is very impressive for the time, was imposed on Chinese society. Lord Shang made a beginning in the standardization of weights and measures.[28] Later this standardization was extended to the length of axles on carts, an extremely important measure in Northern China, where ruts cut deep into the loess. Perhaps even more important was the establishment of uniformity in writing. In the opinion of one distinguished historian these measures rescued the unity of Chinese culture.[29] The Ch'in emperor also appears to have succeeded in getting the control of weapons and the means of violence into his own hands.[30] In this manner a bureaucratic élite based on individual merit or wealth replaced a local hierarchy based on noble birth or territorial possessions.[31]

In addition to standardization, regularity, and uniformity — important elements in any bureaucracy — early Chinese bureaucracy also displayed the more distinctively totalitarian trait of well-developed internal espionage and mutual denunciation. Whoever denounced a "culprit" received, according to the rules, the same reward as he who decapitated an enemy. Apparently the rules provided that a person who cut off one head advanced one degree in rank, while he who cut off two heads advanced two ranks. Possibly the tendency toward a breakdown of the authority of a superior over his inferiors that such an arrangement could be expected to produce was held in check by a system of purely nominal ranks alongside the real offices.[32] In a way that further recalls modern totalitarian practices official functions in the Ch'in empire were divided among two or more offices to enable one to keep watch over the other. As an additional safeguard the emperor appointed inspectors to watch over the acts of provincial authorities.[33]

The main purpose of this bureaucratic control was to direct the energies of Ch'in society to the conquest of other states. The work of Lord Shang helped to make it possible for the Ch'in to embark on the series of conquests that culminated in the proclamation of the first Chinese emperor in 221 B.C. This was neither the first nor the last time in human history that an important economic and social revolution has worked itself out in this manner.

The Ch'in state was unable, however, to focus these energies to the extent that is possible under a modern dictatorship. In addition to the resources of propaganda and terror on a gigantic scale, a twentieth-century dictator is able to manipulate economic incentives and penalties in such a way that even rank and file workers in field and factory will bend their utmost energy to act in accord with the dictator's policies. The economic controls that were suggested or carried out in the Ch'in state and empire had a different character. They were mainly attempts to preserve an agrarian ethic against the erosion of commercial life and luxury. Thus, in the *Book of Lord Shang,* a compilation of different styles and dates, cast in the form of advice to a ruler, one passage urges that the price of meat and wine be made so heavy that merchants and retailers would be few, farmers would be unable to enjoy drinking bouts, and officials would not be able to overeat.[34] In general, says the same source, the ruler ought to make the rich poor and the poor rich, since in this way envy and licentiousness will be held in check and the polity united.[35] All this is trivial in comparison with the machinery a modern state can bring to bear on its inhabitants. Though the life of the Chinese peasant undoubtedly changed markedly under the Ch'in, we can be certain there was no forced uprooting of ancient mores such as the Communists imposed on the Russian peasants during the collectivization of agriculture.

Those who did feel the brunt of Ch'in despotism were

the intellectuals. To my knowledge the land of the mandarin enjoys the doubtful honor of being the first civilized state to engage in book-burning and a mass slaughter of its intellectuals. Traditionally minded elements among scholars who clung to Confucian models helped to express the resentment of the feudal aristocracy dispossessed by the Ch'in rulers. In turn the latter reacted with terrorist acts and the establishment of a rudimentary system of thought control.

One incident, the "Burning of the Books," in 213 B.C., has become famous in Chinese history and is worth reporting in some detail. At a state banquet one of the Confucian scholars addressed the emperor with a speech praising the state of affairs under the earlier dynasties. He attributed the stability of former periods to the rulers' practice of presenting their sons and brothers with fiefs, urging the emperor to copy this practice. Li Ssŭ, an adviser to the Ch'in emperor, who played a role similar to Lord Shang, was present at the banquet. Evidently he saw his opportunity and arose to make a proposal, which though drastic, had its precedents in the history of the Ch'in state.[36] After criticizing the view that the past could furnish political models applicable to the present, Li Ssŭ is reported to have said:

Now that the emperor possesses the whole land and has imposed unity, they [i.e., the Confucian intellectuals] honor the past and hold private consultations. These men who oppose the new laws and commands, as soon as they hear of a new edict, discuss it in accordance with their doctrines. When they are at Court they conceal their resentment, but when they are elsewhere they debate these matters in the public streets and encourage the common people to believe calumnies. This being the case, unless we take action the authority of the sovereign will be abased, the associations of the malcontents will grow powerful. It is necessary to prevent this. Your subject proposes that the histories [of the feudal states], with the exception of that of Ch'in, shall all be burnt. With the exception of those holding the rank of 'Scholars of Great Learning' [a group of 70 scholars appointed by the court] all men in the entire empire who possess copies of [these works] must all take these books to the magistrates to be burnt. Those who dare to discuss and comment [on these works] shall be put to death and their bodies exposed in the market place. Those who praise ancient institutions to decry the present regime shall be exterminated with all the members of their families. Officials who condone breaches of this law shall themselves be implicated in the crime. Thirty days after the publication of this decree all who have not burnt their books will be branded and sent to forced labor on the Great Wall. Those books which shall be permitted are only those which treat of medicine, divination, agriculture, and arboriculture. As for those who wish to study law and administration, let them take the governing officials as their masters.[37]

This speech shows several striking parallels with modern totalitarian thought and practice. One is the fear of "private thinking" that draws on an older tradition to form negative judgments about the contemporary situation. Another is the exception made in favor of a small group of "reliable" court intellectuals, who may have been free to study subversive ideas in order to refute them. Still another similarity is the exclusion of factual scientific information from the political ban, though at times modern totalitarian regimes have encroached on this as well.

In the opinion of specialists it is unlikely that this form of thought control was put into effect in a thorough and rigorous manner.[38] The most striking incident of the use of terror occurred a year later, in 212 B.C., when the emperor ordered more than 460 of the literati to be buried alive. Whether this was a calculated political move or merely the personal whim of an angry despot is no longer clear from the available accounts.[39] In any case, however, such an act would have been perfectly consistent with the dominant political philosophy of the time.

This philosophy is highly significant for our purposes because it shows that under the strains of a changing agrarian order there emerged in ancient China a syndrome of ideas similar to German National Socialist doctrines, which are often interpreted as the death rattle of an advanced industrial society. This Chinese tradition is known under the somewhat misleading name of the School of Law on account of its emphasis on the importance of legal rules, though these ideas could scarcely be more opposite to what modern Westerners mean when they speak of the rule of law. Some of the major ideas of this school can be traced back at least as far as the seventh century B.C.[40] Its membership was largely recruited from "uprooted intellectuals," that is, scholars deprived of their high position in Chinese society by the revolutionary changes of the times. Many of these individuals moved from court to court selling their skills as amoral political advisers to rulers compelled by the circumstances of the day to adopt a ruthless policy of advancing their own power.[41]

The major premise of this philosophy is that a state should seek internal unity through severe discipline in order to become strong and conquer the enemy. This theme recurs in various forms throughout the *Book of Lord Shang*. In a manner characteristic of modern totalitarianism the premise leads to concentration on the power of the state and the rejection of all other values. This is stated quite explicitly:

> The things which the people desire are innumerable, but that from which they benefit is one and the same thing. Unless the people be made one, there is no way to make them attain their desire. . . . Therefore, a country that knows how to produce strength and how to reduce it is said to be "one that attacks the enemy" and is sure to become strong. It bars all private roads for gratifying their ambition . . . it can make the people first do what they hate, in order, thereafter, to reach what they desire, and so their strength will be great.[42]

Concentration on power was combined with a strictly amoral attitude, an embryonic form of amoral rationalism as we know it in modern Western society. The Legalist viewpoint rejected any standard of behavior for the ruler that might constitute a barrier to the pursuit of power, and accepted any action that might be technically efficient. Thus "A country where the virtuous govern the wicked will suffer from disorder, so that it will be dismembered; but a country where the wicked govern the virtuous will be orderly, so that it will become strong."[43] As a natural consequence of this amoral rationalism the Legalists held public opinion in utter contempt.[44] Such contempt, incidentally, indicates that Chinese popular standards of political morality at that time were at least roughly similar to our own. When we say, therefore, that the Chinese Legal School was amoral we are applying not merely a Western standard but a Chinese one.

In accord with this amoral and purely technical rationalism, the Legalists rejected the standards of Chinese antiquity as inapplicable and positively dangerous for the conduct of contemporary affairs.[45] This rejection was, as we have seen, the basis for the "Burning of the Books." It extended beyond the doctrines of antiquity to any form of cultural activity that might conceivably interfere with the political objectives of the state. Here the main fear was that "dangerous thoughts" might percolate through to the people and unsettle them. For this reason high officials were "not allowed to occupy themselves with extensive learning, brilliant discussions and idle living," or to travel about and give the farmers opportunities to "hear of changes." [46] According to another passage, "if [the people] do not prize learning they will be stupid, and being stupid, they will have no interest in outside things." [47]

As the last passage suggests, the Chinese Legalists had a rather negative view of human nature. As a rule people were more likely to be evil than good. Some of this skeptical cynicism derived from the ruler's frequently well-grounded fear of his own bureaucratic servants. In both the Chinese and the Indian despotisms the ruler always faced a difficult problem in preventing venial officials from exploiting the people and thereby stirring up trouble.[48] If the people were stupid and were to be kept that way deliberately, and if officials were either stupid or corrupt or both, by what methods, a modern reader might ask, was the country to be governed? The answer was by clear laws and by a system of rewards and punishments manipulated from above. The emphasis on law is the source of the name Legalist for this viewpoint. "The way to administer a country well, is for the law for the officials to be clear; therefore one does not rely on intelligent and thoughtful men." [49]

As early as the seventh century the Legalist thinkers had based their system on the assumption that two traits were dominant in human nature, greed and the fear of injury. Out of this viewpoint they developed first a doctrine of rewards and punishments suited to their conception of human nature, and later a conception of positive law, crude from our standpoint,[50] but very advanced for the time, in that it contained the vital element of universal standards applicable to all persons irrespective of social status. In this the Legalist tradition constituted a significant break with the past.[51]

As a general principle the Legalists urged that punishments should be severe and rewards light. The contrast, they apparently thought, made the punishments more awe-inspiring.[52] Nevertheless they were able, by means of what seems superficially to be a crude form of dialectical reasoning, to imagine an eventual situation in which rewards and punishments would no longer be necessary.

The way in which a sage administers a state is by unifying rewards, unifying punishments, and unifying education. The effect of unifying rewards is that the army will have no equal; the effect of unifying punishments is that orders will be carried out; the effect of unifying education is that inferiors will obey superiors. Now if one understands rewards, there should be no expense; if one understands punishments there should be no death penalty; if one understands education there should be no changes, and so people would know the business of the people and there would be no divergent customs. The climax in the understanding of rewards is to bring about a condition of having no rewards; the climax in the understanding of punishments is to bring about a condition of having no punishments; the climax in the understanding of education is to bring about a condition of having no education.[53]

Thus the situation toward which the Chinese Legalists wanted to drive mankind is very close to the standardized automatic conformity, empty of all intellectual content, which many thoughtful people see as our present plight in the middle of the twentieth century.

Perhaps such is the inevitable outcome of the line of thought the Legalists pursued. We must also be careful, however, to understand their philosophy in its own historical context. The force of their criticism was directed against a fragmented feudal polity with its emphasis on the allocation of authority and responsibility on the basis of kinship. In its place they wanted to construct a centralized polity in which authority and responsibility were allocated on the basis of objective merit. After the passage just quoted the very next sentence makes this point explicitly: "What I mean by the unifying of rewards is that profits and emoluments, office and rank should be determined exclusively by military merit, and that there should not be different reasons for distributing them." [54] Then the author repeats the familiar warning against the ancient practice whereby the king presented his victorious generals and soldiers with fiefs and against permitting automatic hereditary succession to office.[55] The thinking of the Chinese Legalists did not pass beyond the destruction of the feudal system and its replacement by a bureaucratic one.

Indeed the Chinese Legalists present to us a curious Janus

face. On the one hand they look forward and wish to destroy tradition. On the other hand they look backward toward a simple agrarian society. They were strongly opposed to the merchants and to commercial interests generally as something that would upset the farmers and thereby reduce the military power of the state. This agrarian element in Legalist thinking was also a source of anti-intellectualism. The connection comes out clearly in the following passage:

> If [the people's] attention is devoted to agriculture, then they will be simple, and being simple, they may be made correct. Being perplexed it will be easy to direct them, being trustworthy, they may be used for defence and warfare. . . . Indeed, the people will love their rulers and obey his commandments even to death, if they are engaged in farming morning and evening; but they will be of no use, if they see that glib-tongued, itinerant scholars succeed in being honored in serving the prince, that merchants succeed in enriching their families and that artisans have plenty to live upon.[56]

In "blood and soil" and other slogans Nazism too shows the same mixture of contempt for the people combined with a nostalgic desire to return to the good old days of "healthy" rural life before men were corrupted by the flesh pots of the cities.

Despite the striking quality of these parallels we will be wise to refrain from saying *plus ça change* . . . and reserve judgment on their meaning. Instead we may take leave of China for a briefer sojourn in India. Since many of the important features of ancient Oriental despotism already appear in China, the presentation will merely concentrate on those aspects of the Indian situation that differed from the Chinese one.

If we search in Oriental history for a situation roughly comparable to China in respect to political institutions, territory, and size of population, the best case turns out to be northern India at nearly the same point in time. The latter part of the fourth century B.C. includes the reign of Chandragupta, founder of the Maurya dynasty, who defeated the Greek forces that Alexander had left in India and established a centralized state including all India north of the Narbada as well as Afghanistan. He died about 298 B.C.[57]

The simultaneous nature of Chinese and Indian developments is probably more than a coincidence, though none of the sources I have examined mention any contact or relationship between them. In both cases it is apparent that we have to do with the transition from a quasi-feudal set of loosely organized states to a centralized empire.[58] In India the Maurya empire arose by swallowing other small states in a reaction against threatened conquest. Whether this threat came mainly from the Persians[59] or at a later date from Alexander the Great[60] is a disputed point, but one that is not significant for our purposes. Until very recently historians limited their explanation of the rise of the Maurya to this factor. In 1956 an Indian historian, very much influenced by Marx, put forth an economic explanation. Essentially his argument holds that the rise of a class of traders favored an increase in the king's power, since only the king could protect their property rights and their persons.[61] While this is a point on which the specialists should rightly have the last word, I rather suspect that the author is forcing a preconceived scheme onto the facts. At all events it is by no means as clear that Indian despotism was the outcome of an economic and social revolution as it is in the case of ancient China.

In its major features the structure of the Maurya regime was similar to the imperial bureaucracy under the Ch'in. "The higher classes," says the *Cambridge History of India,* "had not a landowning, but an official, qualification, being entitled for their maintenance to a defined portion of the revenue." [62] The Maurya bureaucracy rested heavily on the army, whose organization was very elaborate and complex for the times.[63] It also had a highly developed system of internal espionage. Especially striking in the Maurya bureaucracy are the security arrangements to prevent the revelation of official secrets, and the devices prescribed as a crude "loyalty check" on its officers. For example, in the *Arthaçastra,* the Indian counterpart of *The Book of Lord Shang,*[64] one of the prescriptions gives the following advice. After the king's chief advisers had been appointed, one high official, acting as a secret agent for the king, should invite the others to a festival. In a pretense of horror at such an act, the king should then arrest all the officials. Next another secret agent of the king, this time a wandering scholar, should whisper in their ears, "The king has taken to evil ways. Let us therefore kill him and put another in his place. That would be pleasant for all of us. How does it seem to you?" Whoever refused the suggestion was deemed worthy of trust. The *Arthaçastra* described several variations on this device, each appropriate to a particular kind of official.[65]

In economic affairs Maurya policy was very different from that of the Ch'in. The state encouraged and protected merchants and artisans. The latter organized themselves into guilds that created their own rules to govern their members' activity.[66] According to the *Arthaçastra,* the state regulated prices on the markets, sometimes on behalf of the buyer, sometimes the seller. The state also engaged in important economic activities directly. It had a monopoly of mining, managed the royal forests, and operated vast establishments for the collection and storage of taxes in kind.[67] There may also have been a system of crown villages, or colonists sent out to clear vacant lands under royal supervision. Any one who failed to cultivate the land assigned to him would lose it.[68] An aura of uncertainty, however, hangs over all of these institutions. In the *Arthaçastra* it is difficult to determine whether the material describes the actual practice of a real Indian despot or merely presents a detailed "policy recommendation" purporting to demonstrate how *any* ruler might become and remain a successful despot. Even if the ideas expressed in this document correspond only very roughly to actual practice, the appearance of such ideas in the pre-industrial world constitutes important evidence for our problem.

It is also difficult to determine the impact of this bureaucratic structure on the underlying population. If the crown colonies mentioned above ever existed on a large scale, they would of course represent a high degree of effective central control over the day-to-day economic life of the population. There are several indications that the central authorities made strenuous efforts to know everything that was happening in both the town and the countryside. In the cities an official, whose name significantly means cow-herd, was expected to keep records of each group of ten, twenty, or forty households. He was expected to report the caste, family, and occupation of every man and woman of these households as well as their income and expenditure. In the countryside the village headman was subordinated through an elaborate chain of command to the central administration in the capital.[69] There are some indications in the *Arthaçastra* that the spy system may have extended beyond the bureaucracy and the towns to penetrate the roots of village life.[70]

From these facts alone one might conclude merely that there existed an elaborate system of registering what the population was doing without any attempt to influence or control its behavior. It is hardly likely, however, that the state collected this information merely out of curiosity. There are indications that, as under the Ch'in, and for that matter under modern totalitarian regimes too, the ruler used this system of reporting, supervision, and espionage to break up any pre-existing social units that could serve as foci of resistance to his power. The uses to which these devices were put appear clearly from a passage in the *Arthaçastra* on the technique of breaking up the remnants of tribal organization.

Agents provocateurs should gain access to all these tribes, discover the possible sources of jealousy, hatred, contention among them, should disseminate the seeds of progressive dissension. Let those of higher rank (within the tribe) be discouraged from eating at a common table with and marriage with those of lower standing. Tribesmen of lower rank should, on the other hand, be instigated to (insist upon) commensality and intermarriage with the higher. The lesser should be provoked to claim equality of status in family, prowess. . . . Public decisions and tribal custom should be brought to dissolution by insistence upon the contrary. Litigation should be turned into a fight by the (king's paid) bravi who, at night, injure property, beasts, or men. . . . On all occasions of (such intra-tribal) conflict, the king should support the weaker party with (his own) funds and army, should instigate them to annihilate their opponents. . . . Thus he might proceed against the tribes to become the sole absolute ruler (over them, as over the rest of the land).[71]

It is a safe guess that the same technique was used in other areas of Indian society for the same purposes. At the same time we must beware of reading the present back into the past and attributing overmuch efficiency and effectiveness to this ancient form of despotism. The *Arthaçastra* frequently laments the difficulties of controlling the king's servants, which certainly must have been very great in as large an area as this before the days of modern rapid communications. Bureaucratic agents of the king were easily seduced into becoming part of the society which the royal authority was endeavoring to control. We may conclude safely that beneath this bureaucracy, and only somewhat permeated by it, the ancient structures of kinship, village, and caste continued to guide daily life, though the details of their operation are uncertain at this distant point in time.

We may close this interpretation of Indian despotism with a few remarks on its political philosophy as revealed in the *Arthaçastra*. This work displays as its central trait the same kind of amoral rationalism, interested only in successful political technique, as that we found in the *Book of Lord Shang*. The *Arthaçastra* has a somewhat more formal, abstract, and generalizing character. Sometimes it gives off a rather bookish air, as of a writer proud of his own cleverness, but lacking any firsthand contact with politics. In all these respects it resembles some currents of modern social science, particularly those associated with psychological warfare. Indeed there is little sardonic exaggeration in the assertion that most of the principles of contemporary psychological and political warfare and even their practical application were already known and formulated by the authors of the *Arthaçastra* and the *Book of Lord Shang*. The most conspicuous difference between the ancient and the modern traditions is the absence in the older one of any conception of stirring up and organizing the masses to achieve political objectives.

The political passivity of the masses constitutes one of the distinctive traits of Indian and Chinese despotism. At the same time the "entrance of the masses onto the stage of history" cannot be regarded as the consequence of industrialism. They already played an active part in Greece, Rome, and Byzantium. We shall encounter them in our next case, Calvinist Geneva.

IV

For the student of modern totalitarianism the rise of Calvinism in Geneva is illuminating on several grounds. In the history of Geneva it is possible to trace the transformation of a democracy into a totalitarian regime, though neither the beginning state nor the final one correspond altogether with what these terms usually mean today. Furthermore, the main impact of Calvin's dictatorship was on the daily habits and thoughts of the population rather than on the city's formal political structure. On this account Calvin's regime sheds light on the repressive social conformity that is widely regarded as a totalitarian consequence of industrialism, even in formally democratic states.

The social structure of Geneva a hundred years before Calvin's appearance on the scene was about what one would expect of a late medieval city that was a flourishing center of commerce. Its population at the beginning of the fifteenth century is estimated as somewhere between 7,000 and 10,000 persons.[72] This population was divided into four major groups. At the bottom were the ordinary inhabitants who had no political privileges and were merely tolerated. Next came the bourgeoisie proper. These had the right to vote. Some had purchased this right; a few had received it without payment; the rest were children of the bourgeoisie. Strictly speaking, only the latter were citizens, though the franchise was not confined to them until later. Next there was the feudal nobility, possessors of fiefs in the neighboring territory. Finally another important and influential group was the clergy, drawn from all levels of the population. Considerable mixture prevailed among the nobility and the wealthier elements among the bourgeoisie.[73] Except for the assertion that the clergy contained no less then 300 persons,[74] we are not informed about the size of these social divisions, though it is a safe guess that the ordinary inhabitants were the largest.

Political power in Geneva was shared, at first rather peacefully among the clergy, the feudal aristocracy, led by the House of Savoy, and the bourgeoisie. During most of the fifteenth century the Genevans displayed no hostility to the

House of Savoy. The duke was often a relative of the bishop.[75] Naturally these were not completely homogeneous groups, and there were conflicts of interest within them as well as among them. Internal divisions were particularly important within the clergy, at whose apex stood the bishop. Since the bishop was frequently absent, the Chapter, composed of canons who elected the bishop, often enjoyed much of the substance of power.[76] The conflict of interests within the clergy played a part in the delicate balance of powers among the three leading sections of Genevan society. Thus the authority of the clergy was balanced by that of the syndics, four in number, who were elected twice each year by the assembled bourgeoisie. The bishop, and his subordinate officer, the *vidomne,* a military and judicial official, gave oath before the syndics to respect the rights and electoral privileges of the city. Though these clerical officials alone had the right to judge important criminal cases and to inflict the death penalty, every member of the bourgeoisie arrested by one of the bishop's subordinates could appeal to be taken before the syndics within twenty-four hours.[77] The picture that emerges from the historians' accounts is one in which feudal custom filled in the interstices left by the formal confusion of powers, and whose institutions worked by and large to secure the liberties of the citizens. About the ordinary inhabitants there is less information, though no indication of active discontent. Like the democratic city-states of antiquity, Geneva was really an oligarchy, but one in which power was considerably diffused. The balance of power among the leading segments of Genevan society was complemented by the policy of playing off against one another the principal powers external to the city: pope, emperor, king of France, and the Swiss Leagues.

To the extent that the preceding analysis is correct, the problem of accounting for the emergence of Calvin's dictatorship becomes in large measure one of explaining the disintegration of this balance. It was destroyed before Calvin ever set foot in Geneva. To recount the series of political moves and countermoves that form the history of its destruction would take us too far afield. Essentially what destroyed the balance were the efforts of each participant — the bishop, the bourgeoisie, and the House of Savoy — to increase its influence at the expense of the others. Meanwhile outside powers, particularly the Protestant city of Bern, fished in the troubled waters for reasons of their own. Bern's emissaries introduced Protestant doctrine into Geneva for the first time in 1526.[78] In the course of events Bern became the only foreign ally to which the Genevan bourgeoisie could turn in its struggle with the House of Savoy. During the later stages of the contest the bishop in despair turned to the House of Savoy for help against Protestantism. The immediate result was to put the Council, as leader of the bourgeoisie, which had been endeavoring to hold a neutral position, along with other uncertain elements, into the opposite camp. The ultimate consequence was to destroy the power of the bishop, who soon ceased to be an effective contestant.[79]

In these events one can see some of the structural weaknesses of any social system based upon a balance of competing interest groups. Such a balance confronts the groups who participate in it with a situation where it is necessary to run in order to stand still, that is, to get more power merely in order to stay even with one's rivals. Cumulative pressures generated in this fashion may sooner or later destroy the balance by eliminating one of the contestants. This seems to have happened in Geneva. As a matter of theory one can see that a balance-of-power situation could generate rivalries even when there were no conflicts of material interest among the members of the balance. In actual practice, of course, economic and doctrinal rivalries as well as a host of others are in most cases, and perhaps all, intertwined with the conflicts generated by a balance-of-power situation. To disentangle these elements in the political struggles that preceded Calvin's rule in Geneva would be a very difficult but a worthwhile task requiring specialized knowledge of the sources. Secondary accounts give me the impression that economic conflicts did not play a major role. Instead it appears that the balance of power among clergy, feudal elements, and bourgeoisie brought about its own destruction to a very large extent through the mechanics of its own operation.

The religious conflict in the course of time did become a very real one. During this preliminary period the position of the liberal bourgeoisie became increasingly untenable. They found themselves more and more in the very difficult situation of moderate democrats trying to uphold abstract ideals of law and order at a time when passions run deep. Significant also in relation to modern problems is the loss of any strong commitment to the old order. By the second quarter of the sixteenth century whatever emotional attachment there may have been to Genevan institutions was largely replaced by habit. This situation gave a tremendous advantage to those who challenged the status quo. The challengers knew what they wanted to destroy; the defenders were uncertain about the value of what they wished to keep. The absence of anyone able or willing to undertake the intellectual defense of Catholicism is particularly striking.[80] In its ineffective attempts to preserve order the Council gave scarcely any indication that its members felt deeply about the old order. For this reason, among others, it played into the hands of the revolutionary reformers.[81]

One further factor behind the success of Calvinism remains to be discussed. We may call it the return of respectability, for lack of any other suitable term. In the fifteenth century Geneva was from all accounts a fun-loving city, in which the pleasures of the bed, the bottle, the table, and the gaming board were available in abundance.[82] In the year 1459, fifty years before the birth of Calvin, the Chapter issued the first recorded police regulation aimed at limiting such pleasures. Among other provisions it ordered the city prostitutes to choose a "queen," an arrangement that was to enable the authorities to regulate prostitution more closely. Such a queen had in fact existed as early as 1413. By the new regulation she was obliged to take an oath on the Holy Gospel that she would perform her task faithfully.[83] This regulation was the first of a long series of municipal acts, all antedating Calvin, that were directed toward the protection of female virtue, the restriction of concubinage, and the elimination of gambling.

In other words, Calvin's austere doctrines must have found a receptive audience in some segments of Genevan society. Except for passing remarks to the effect that much of his authority derived from the foreigners who flocked into the city following his victory,[84] the historians do not tell us from what sections of Geneva society the Reformation drew its support. By a process of elimination, however, we may conclude that before Calvin's time support came mainly from those without the franchise. The higher bourgeoisie, as suggested by the efforts of the Council to remain neutral, did not respond favorably in the early stages, while the clergy and nobility were in active opposition. As far as I am aware, no one has made a detailed study of the reasons why the lower strata flocked to Calvin's support. We may be sure, however, that virtuous envy of those who enjoyed the pleasures of the flesh played an important part.

The arrival of Calvin's demagogic predecessor, William Farel, in the autumn of 1532, appears to have been the first step toward active control and mobilization of popular elements. At first Farel's rough and insulting manner produced a popular reaction of disgust that favored the Catholics.[85] But by the summer of 1535 Farel at the head of a mob forced his way into one of the leading churches in the midst of a service, marched up to the altar and took possession of the church. This tactic he repeated on several occasions. Finally he marched into the main church, St. Peter's, to the pealing of the tower bells. At this point the Council tried to intervene with an order to forbid Farel's further preaching in St. Peter's. Then, according to a contemporary Protestant source, "God scorned the counsels of the elders and roused the children of Geneva against them." In the afternoon of the same day a howling mob of "little children" stormed the church, and broke up the service. This was the signal for general pillage and destruction of church ornaments, in which many valuable works of art perished.[86] Calvin's ultimate victory was not far off.

It is time now to turn to Calvin himself and the doctrines that he endeavored to put into effect in Geneva. Since these doctrines have been the subject of extensive scholarly discussion, it is only necessary for our purposes to review very briefly their quasi-totalitarian features.* Calvin's objective was to establish a Christian state. The real model for this state was the Israelite theocracy at the time of the kings.[87] In this feature there might possibly be an historical link between ancient Oriental despotism and modern totalitarianism. However, Calvin's doctrine as such completely lacks the explicit, amoral, political rationalism that was such a prominent feature in both the Chinese and Indian versions of Oriental despotism during the periods discussed.

As formulated in the *Institutio Religionis Christianae,* published in 1536, Calvin's doctrine constituted a rejection of both reason and historical tradition as guides for human conduct and as bases for human society. In this as well as other aspects of his doctrine Calvin remained adamant and consistent to the day of his death.[89] For Calvin the scripture

---

* In justice to Calvin we must note that his doctrine also contained certain ideas that were later to form an important part of the Western democratic and anti-absolutist tradition. For example, in regard to civil government he asserts that all law contains an element of reason and equity. To this he adds that "Toutes les loix du monde de quelque affaire que ce soit, doyvent revenir à une mesme équité." [88]

in a very literal sense constituted the unique and necessary source of belief. For him no historical development existed in the growth of Christian doctrine. He saw no need for human reason any more than for historical tradition in the interpretation of the letter of the Bible.[90] God has imparted to us what it is pious to know. To wish to know more would be presumption.[91] Humanity exists only as a means for the glorification of the divine majesty of God.[92] This praise of God must appear in the form of the perfected morality of the community.[93] Here is the justification for the community's detailed and tyrannical interference with private life.

The basic premise of the entire system is the doctrine of predestination. Calvin divides mankind into those chosen by God for eternal life and those condemned to eternal damnation. God's choice is purely arbitrary and bears no relation to people's behavior. In Calvin's own words,

Nous appelons Prédestination: le conseil éternel de Dieu, par lequel il a déterminé ce qu'il vouloit faire d'un chacun homme. Car il ne les crée pas tous en pareille condition: mais ordonne les uns à vie éternelle, les autres à éternelle damnation. Ainsi selon la fin à laquelle est crée l'homme, nous disons qu'il est prédestiné à mort ou à vie.[94]

The view that people are saved for "good behavior" Calvin explicitly rejects as a form of haggling. As to God, "il sauve de son bon plaisir ceux que bon luy semble, et . . . ce n'est pas pour rendre salaire." [95] Calvinism is thus rigidly determinist. Yet it is a determinism that provides psychological support for an active attitude toward life and the affairs of this world. As Communism demonstrates, and perhaps also the early states of Islam, a determinist philosophy does not in and by itself produce a fatalistic passive attitude. Instead it may have quite the opposite consequence.

Calvin's opportunity to put his ideas into practice did not come until five years after the publication of the *Institutes*. Then, in 1541, he was recalled to Geneva from exile. For some fourteen years his program encountered severe resistance, met by executions and arrests. This period we must pass over in order to examine the full-blown theocratic dictatorship of his later years. Historians tell us that by the year 1555 opposition must have seemed hopeless, as its leaders were by then all in jail or exile.[96] Nine years remained until Calvin's death, in 1564, during which time he continued to exert every effort to put his conceptions into practice. Calvin's dictatorship made no attempt at a centralized control of the economy. Such an attempt would have been foreign to the spirit of his system. On the other hand, a complex and subtle system of political, intellectual, and social controls maintained his power.

Changes in the formal structure of the government were relatively few. Representative institutions created by the Geneva bourgeoisie continued to function, though in a transformed spirit. Calvin's return in 1541 already signified the victory of the ecclesiastical over the secular arm of the community.[97] But Calvin understood that he still required the help of the civil authority, which he placed under the tutelage of the Council. This body he made undergo an examination on questions of faith as if it were a college of theologians.[98] To be sure, in 1560 a set of decrees was adopted in the name of the syndics and other state bodies that made certain constitutional changes under the guise of clarifying existing rules. Their effect, however, was limited to relatively minor changes in the franchise, which increased the influence of Calvin's supporters.[99] In general, civil and secular authority supported one another. The state confirmed the election of ministers chosen according to ecclesiastical requirements. Correspondingly the church supervised the doctrinal "loyalty" and acceptability of the secular officials.[100]

Even elections continued. In 1559 the Council decreed that a member of the clergy should address the people before elections so that they might approach this civic task in a pious frame of mind and permit themselves to be led by God. Calvin himself usually appeared at electoral gatherings to recall the great events of the time and to remind the citizens of their duties with the fervor and earnestness of an Old Testament prophet.[101] It was regarded as a conspiracy to speak in opposition to the list of candidates presented by the clergy.[102] To the sound of trumpets it was announced to the populace in 1560 that henceforth all citizens and inhabitants were forbidden to discuss public matters except in the presence of the Council, since much discussion produced false rumors and threatened the security of the city.[103] Under all these conditions it is scarcely surprising that the elections produced officials eminently satisfactory to the clergy.[104]

These electoral manipulations foreshadow the plebiscitary character of modern dictatorship and distinguish the Calvinist regime from Oriental despotism. Distinctive Western elements also appear in the character of Calvin's own position in the Geneva theocracy. He expressly avoided any outward symbol of his own superiority. He made a point of treating his colleagues formally as equals. To avoid jealousies Calvin proposed in 1558 that all ecclesiastical salaries should be equal.[105] On the other hand, Calvin's voice was decisive. Every important issue in Geneva's foreign and domestic problems came to him for decision. The Council, formerly outstanding for its statesmanship, finally became completely dependent on Calvin.[106]

The most important structural change was the creation of the Consistorium. Originally conceived by Calvin merely as a device to supervise marital questions,[107] the Consistorium developed into the major center of political, moral, and religious control. One historian treats it as a replacement for the institution of the bishop, which no longer existed.[108] After 1555 it became more and more the central institution that gave both tone and direction to the political and social life of Geneva. Gradually it gained the power to criticize the administration of justice and the decisions of the Council.[109] As a result the Council tried to outdo the Consistorium in severity.[110]

The Consistorium performed the services of a secret police and moral censorship. Its activities in this pre-industrial age show many striking parallels to modern practices. According to Kampschulte, nothing escaped the knowledge of the Consistorium. Its members knew everything that took place in clerical and civil life. What they did not find out for themselves in the relatively small community of Geneva, they learned through informants and spies, a service into which the refugees from France entered will-

ingly. They learned of every utterance with heretical overtones, even when it took place in private conversation. They
knew how often a person went to church, what his favorite
reading matter was, and if his expenses exceeded his income. They informed themselves about the price of the
wine he drank and the remarks that he made when
traveling outside Geneva on business. If the Council wished
to know the names of the lazy characters and gluttons in
the city of Geneva, the Consistorium provided a list that
was complete beyond reproach.[111]

The impact of Calvin's system of controls fell heavily
upon the daily life of the citizens, indeed far more heavily
than did the control system in any of the cases discussed
previously. As early as 1546 the law prohibited the favorite
pastimes of Geneva — feasts, dancing, dice, and ball games.
It decreed the cut of people's clothes and the style of their
shoes. After complaints by the pastors about the way in which
women tried to attract attention, the Council gave in and
decreed the amount and kind of silverware and dishes
that might be used at mealtime, as well as the costumes
that women might wear. "The last fortress behind which
feminine coquetry might entrench itself was ground
down." [112]

Detailed measures were taken to ensure the dominance
of Calvinistic beliefs. Marriage could take place only between believers, lest the partnership should undermine the
faith of one of its members. A believer was held responsible
not only for his own behavior but that of his family.[113]
On this score Calvin himself apparently constituted an exception, for the breath of scandal did not touch him when

his sister-in-law was caught in adultery with Calvin's own servant in Calvin's own house. The master merely consoled himself with the thought that now his brother could get a divorce.[114]

Moreover, it was forbidden to mark Catholic holidays by fasting. Those who tried to do so were warned to eat meat or face the consequences before the courts. The Consistorium repressed other Catholic rituals, particularly forbidding the population to pray for the deceased, to kneel on a grave, or to throw a handful of dirt upon a coffin. In 1555 the Consistorium invited a man to appear before it who had lit a candle before the corpse of his child.[115]

Thus the Consistorium did its best to make sure that people gave more than formal allegiance to Calvin's doctrine. Calling people up for formal interrogation, it asked in effect, "Have you really given up Mass? Do you still believe in good works? In the saints? In prayers for the deceased?" [116] As part of the check on the purity of doctrine the Consistorium also organized its own version of the Inquisition in regard to books.[117]

The Calvinists also betrayed pronounced anxiety lest competing Protestant sects, among them the carriers of communist ideas, might gain a foothold among the common folk. Already in 1537 a decree had condemned the members of one such sect to remain in perpetual banishment, threatening them with the death penalty if they returned.[118] Behind all the measures, whether directed against rival beliefs or the routine activities of citizens, stood the power of the executioner. Nor did the regime fail to resort to his services where it encountered severe opposition.[119]

The reaction of the people of Geneva to this forerunner of modern repressive society is both enlightening and depressing. Ineffective individual acts of opposition occurred rather frequently even at the height of Calvin's power. These were easily suppressed. To cite one example, a certain Jacques Simon was put in prison for having exclaimed "baboon!" to someone who woke him up during a sermon, adding that "he would go to church willingly if they preached the word of God there." [120] A few managed to leave Geneva because they could not "kiss Calvin's slippers." [121] By and large, however, Calvin and his followers evidently succeeded in diffusing over Geneva a miasma of fearful hostility to any curiosity about new ideas or differences of opinions. Like the Bolsheviks, the true Calvinists had a deadly fear of error and its social consequences, believing every error must be nipped in the bud.[122] Gradually criticism from within the community died down. Even opposition elements became permeated with Calvinist convictions. So today also, strongly anti-Communist refugees from the USSR display many Soviet elements in their thinking. Finally, certain aspects of the doctrine, even the theory of predestination, gained some popularity. There was pride in belonging to those chosen by God, much as there is pride among some Russians at being allegedly selected as the agents of a great historical transformation. In the sober city of Geneva today even the casual tourist of the twentieth century may still be struck with the strong traces of the Calvinist impact upon its inhabitants.

V

On examining even the limited range of evidence brought together here, we can conclude that the basic conception of centralized totalitarianism, as well as its most important instruments, arose prior to industrialism and independently of industrialism. Men did not have to wait for the industrial revolution to invent schemes of universal salvation that would justify coercing their fellows onto the path of Messianic conquest. Nor did mankind have to wait this long to invent social institutions that multiply the authority of a leader to make the coercion effective.

Let us look briefly at these pre-industrial systems to see what common factors exist in their origins, their methods of control, and their doctrines. There are, of course, significant differences between pre-industrial and twentieth-century repressive systems, which we will consider and evaluate later.

The situations that favor the growth of totalitarian institutions recur intermittently throughout history. In the cases discussed in this essay the major common element appears to be the occurrence of some threat to the society or to an important part of it. The source of the threat seems to vary and cannot always be explained in terms of economic changes.[123] Certainly it is clear in Western history that in many cases a severely repressive regime may emerge in response to economic changes, either from the attempt of a privileged class to prevent a basic redistribution of power and authority, or from the efforts of less privileged classes to force through reforms. But the evidence does not warrant the conclusion that economic factors are always basic to the rise of dictatorial regimes. There is scarcely any sign of this factor in Calvinist Geneva, where we perceive the gradual undermining of a "democratically" balanced society in the face of a religious revolution. The importance of economic factors is very dubious in the Indian case too, where the threat of foreign conquest appears to have been the main reason for the growth of the Maurya system. Finally, in the cases of witchcraft in nonliterate societies, economic factors certainly do not offer a universal explanation. Possibly the apparent absence of significant economic factors in the cases mentioned is due to defects in the sources, though this seems unlikely since other factors do account moderately well for what happened. It thus seems more satisfactory on both empirical and logical grounds to consider economic change as a special case under the more general category of threat and danger which is the main element present at the birth of dictatorial institutions.*

In pre-industrial societies, as in modern times, the purpose of centralized political controls is to coordinate as far as possible the activities of a society in the pursuit of a single goal, such as conquest, defense against an enemy, the prevention or the promotion of social change. A bureaucracy with tentacles that penetrate and regulate all other institutions — economic organizations, military forces, religious groups, the family, the neighborhood, and others — constitutes an indispensable instrument in this attempt at

---

* It would be interesting but outside the scope of this essay to search for historical cases in which repressive institutions or doctrines did *not* develop in response to an internal or external threat.

coordination. Espionage and denunciation are an equally necessary device for keeping both the bureaucratic instrument itself in line and for checking opposition among the general population. Terror and thought control complete the picture in both pre-industrial and modern varieties of totalitarianism.

As we have seen, such institutions existed in a well-developed form in both ancient India and China. Without any attempt to control the economy, but reaching further into private life, the same configuration occurs in Calvin's Geneva. This unhappy city also presents the spectacle of a pre-industrial society with a flourishing system of sham democracy, with its "freedom" and "equality" defined by despotic authority. Sham democracy supplements more mechanical methods of coercion by attracting popular support. It is, to my knowledge, strictly a European institution. Already familiar under the early Roman Empire, it cannot be regarded as a product of the modern world. Yet it marks a step along the way toward the full development of widespread acceptance of the illusion of freedom for its substance. We shall see later how this tendency is related to the effects of industrialism.

The building-blocks and, in some cases, the entire framework of totalitarian controls existed before industrialism. What industrialism has done is to make these structures incomparably more efficient. Among the control devices themselves, the main innovation produced by contemporary totalitarian movements is the single mass party, led by the dictator, and composed of a small percentage of the population. From the broad perspective of an evolutionary standpoint toward human society this change turns out to be merely a refinement on sham democracy, designed to entrap a larger proportion of the population.[124]

Let us now turn to the doctrines, comparing older with modern totalitarian beliefs. Of the cases examined, the ideas of the Legalists in ancient China display the closest resemblance to modern doctrines of centralized totalitarianism. First of all, there is an emphasis on a strong state to the exclusion of other social aims and values. Accompanying this is a strictly amoral and technically rational attitude toward political behavior. Anything that strengthens the ruler's power is good, and that is the end of it. Consistent with this amoral rationalism is the rejection of preceding tradition where it presents images and values that conflict with current objectives. Another important part of the doctrine is the belief that the mass of the people is essentially stupid and should be kept that way. Together with the stress on the virtue of an agrarian life, such an attitude would seem to characterize many reactionary regimes trying to prevent new classes from rising to power. Finally, the Legalists imagined a "dialectical heaven" where repression, after accomplishing its purposes, would no longer be necessary. The same emphasis on the power of the ruler and on amoral rationalism also characterizes the *Arthaçastra,* the guidebook for the ancient Indian princes. In Calvin's doctrine, which lacks the explicit amoral rationalism so prominent in the Oriental theories, the attempt to establish an ideal society here on earth provides the justification for terror and spying. With the Chinese Legalists the doctrine of Calvin also shares the rejection of any tradition or way of thought, including reason, that could constitute a basis for criticizing the proposed ideal.

The parallels to modern totalitarian thoughtways are too obvious to require extensive elaboration. It is clear that we have here a substantial congruence between whole systems of thought, not an accidental overlap between discrete and secondary ideas. Both Communism and National Socialism display amoral and merely technical rational attitudes toward politics, stress the power of the state, reject traditions that could provide a basis for criticizing their doctrines, and put forth the notion (weaker in the case of National Socialism) of some final state when repression will no longer be necessary.

The main difference between these pre-industrial and modern doctrines is connected with the historical stage reached by the notion of reason. About the modern ones we can say that reason has been degraded to a technical instrument for choosing between methods while it has been deprived of the power to appraise ends. Since the conception of reason had not developed very far in Chinese and Indian philosophy,[125] we cannot really speak of a degradation of reason in these cases. The case of Calvinism is more complicated. To summarize it with the utmost brevity we might say that reason cannot comprehend the will of God, but that it is legitimate to apply reason to certain secular affairs.[126] Calvin's position therefore comes closer to the twentieth-century degradation of reason.

As we turn from the doctrine and control apparatus of these pre-industrial regimes to examine their impact on the underlying population, a major difference between older forms and contemporary totalitarianism strikes us at once. The controls of modern totalitarianism cut far deeper into the social fabric than has ever been the case in history. In this respect they are indeed unique.

The rulers in some ancient despotisms obviously would have liked to control the lives of their subjects right down to the last detail if they could have done so. China is the clearest example among the cases discussed in this essay. Without modern industrial technology, deeply effective controls were impossible. The economy had to be left to run itself, mainly along traditional lines. The Chinese peasant planted certain crops because it was customary to do so, not because a government decree ordered him to do so. For older despotisms it was difficult to manipulate even indirectly the economic situation facing their rural subjects, which any modern government, including a democratic one, can do comparatively easily. Thus in ancient India and China the life of the subjects continued for the most part to flow in the familiar channels dug by the ancient usages of religion, kinship, and the village. In contrast, in Calvin's Geneva, private life was subject to a pervasive interference, but the Genevan community was a relatively small state and on this important score different from both modern totalitarian and large pre-industrial regimes. Though the subject under ancient despotism might feel considerable loyalty to a distant emperor, he was likely to resent the ruler if tax burdens and military obligations were heavy, as they usually were under the extreme forms of despotism. While the same resentments, and others as well, also exist in a modern totalitarian state, it is safe to conclude that the subject's involvement in ancient despotism was very much less than under a Hitler or a Stalin.

It is at the level of popular response and participation, therefore, that twentieth-century totalitarian regimes differ most sharply from their pre-industrial predecessors. Not all of this difference is necessarily due to the greater capacity of the modern totalitarian government to mold the minds and hearts of its subjects through propaganda, terror, or more subtle rewards and punishments. As many writers on "mass society" have pointed out, there is a recognizable trend in popular attitudes and sentiments toward passive acceptance or approval of the enlarged role of the governing authorities. Such attitudes among the people contribute an important share to the effectiveness of twentieth-century totalitarianism.

It is then easy to perceive the possibility that a new historical form, a decentralized and diffuse system of repression more or less willingly accepted by the mass of the population, may be slowly coming into sight over the horizon. To me this prospect is far more terrifying than the fantasies of a *1984,* since George Orwell's imaginary society was maintained by gadgets rather than by people. If such a society ever comes, it will deserve the label "totalitarian" far more than any of the systems of centralized repression so far known to history because it will rest on the spontaneous support of nearly the total population. Even though there are indications of such a development in the present situation, here as well as abroad, there is no reason to believe that it is inevitable. By spelling out the characteristics of popular totalitarianism in its extreme or ideal form and soberly examining the forces that favor its development, we may help to avoid such a fate.

We may begin by asking if popular totalitarianism has any historical antecedents. While they are harder to discern than the analogues of centralized totalitarian dictatorships, perhaps because of our recent experience and preoccupation with the latter, it is possible to make out the signs of a continuous evolutionary series leading up to the present stage. A few highlights in this series will illustrate the idea that decentralized repression is not something totally new or associated solely with modern industrialism.

Earlier in this essay we discussed certain similarities between witchcraft and modern totalitarian movements, noticing that witchcraft is in some societies a diffuse form of socially acceptable aggression against unusual or nonconforming individuals. How the victim differs from the norm varies considerably. In many cases he may be a marginal person with little or no prestige. In some, on the other hand, he may have some attribute, such as wealth, that the society values. Evidently, then, some aspects of decentralized and diffuse repression occur during a very early stage of human history.

A similar seedling of popular totalitarianism appears in the Greek city-state, in the form of anti-intellectualism. As is well known, Athenian democracy often treated its most distinguished citizens with vindictive hatred. Here, in contrast with many forms of witchcraft, folk aggression found its victims almost entirely among people of creative or superior ability. The judgment of the famous Swiss historian, Jacob Burckhardt, brings out the features that are relevant for our purpose. "Ostracism," he says, "is an invention of the ambitious mass [Strebermasse]. . . . Certainly never in the whole history of the world has mediocrity enjoyed such an outstanding flash of insight; it hid itself ceremoniously behind popular feeling." [127] In these sentences there is no doubt a touch of Burckhardt's own rejection of modern society. Yet the Greeks themselves in their criticisms of anti-intellectual attitudes in Athenian democracy definitely anticipate modern attacks on the cult of mediocrity.

Deeply rooted religious sentiments were an important source of the widespread antagonism toward the political and intellectual leaders of the republic. Many Athenians bitterly resented rational probings into religious beliefs as well as any public signs of disrespect for them. Aristophanes constantly appeals to the "sound instincts" of a "healthy peasantry" against the queries and "fancy theories" of a Socrates. These conservative and rural sentiments fused with those of urban elements in search of quick riches — Burckhardt's *Strebermasse* — to produce an ugly strain of anti-intellectualism in this home of one of the greatest flowerings of Western thought.

Fortunately for Greek civilization and for us the destructive force inherent in this attitude lacked political direction and hence was largely ineffective. Folk resentment and folk piety could be siphoned off into relatively harmless channels — the theater, the games, and festivals. Under the Romans the crueler aspects of folk aggression similarly found an outlet in the amphitheater. During the Middle Ages, however, new and more savage elements from the Jewish Apocalyptic tradition and from Christianity again swelled the stream of decentralized repression. Messianic movements, marked by incredible ferocity, sprang up frequently among the more distressed populations of the towns, bathing many parts of Europe in blood.[128] The Jews were usually the first victims, one of history's most tragic ironies since the notion of a Messiah who would avenge their misfortunes seems to have originated among this unfortunate people.

The demoniacal current of folk thinking and folk behavior obviously continues into the modern world, although it receded temporarily during the eighteenth and nineteenth centuries in some parts of Europe. Marx could even reach the conclusion that the urban masses under the new and vastly altered conditions of his day would soon eliminate the last remnants and causes of human misery and irrational aggression. More conservative thinkers, however, foresaw possible obstacles to the fulfillment of this optimistic hope.

Alexis de Tocqueville was perhaps the first thinker to see clearly that even if the more violent repression of tyrants and mobs receded into the background, there remained in modern society more subtle and equally effective limits on individual freedom. Written more than a hundred years ago, his famous pages on "the tyranny of the majority" stand today as a penetrating description of the mechanics of popular totalitarianism. They deserve extended quotation:

> It is in the examination of the exercise of thought in the United States that we clearly perceive how far the power of the majority surpasses all the powers with which we are acquainted in Europe.

Thought is an invisible and subtle power that mocks all the efforts of tyranny. At the present time the most absolute monarchs in Europe cannot prevent certain opinions hostile to their authority from circulating in secret through their dominions and even in their courts. It is not so in America; as long as the majority is still undecided, discussion is carried on; but as soon as its decision is irrevocably pronounced, everyone is silent, and the friends as well as the opponents of the measure unite in assenting to its propriety. The reason for this is perfectly clear: no monarch is so absolute as to combine all the powers of society in his own hands and to conquer all opposition, as a majority is able to do, which has the right both of making and of executing the laws.

I know of no country in which there is so little independence of mind and real freedom of discussion as in America. . . .

In America the majority raises formidable barriers around the liberty of opinion; within these barriers an author may write what he pleases, but woe to him if he goes beyond them. Not that he is in danger of an auto-da-fé, but he is exposed to continued obloquy and persecution. His political career is closed forever, since he has offended the only authority that is able to open it. Every sort of compensation, even that of celebrity, is refused to him. Before making public his opinions he thought he had sympathizers; now it seems to him that he has none any more since he has revealed himself to everyone; then those who blame him criticize loudly and those who think as he does keep quiet and move away without courage. He yields at length, overcome by the daily effort which he has to make, and subsides into silence, as if he felt remorse for having spoken the truth.

Fetters and headsmen were the coarse instruments that tyranny formerly employed; but the civilization of our age has perfected despotism itself, though it seemed to have nothing to learn. . . . The master no longer says: "You shall think as I do or you shall die"; but he says: "You are free to think differently from me and to retain your life, your property, and all that you possess; but you are henceforth a stranger among your people. You may retain your civil rights, but they will be useless to you, for you will never be chosen by your fellow citizens if you solicit their votes; and they will affect to scorn you if you ask for their esteem. You will remain among men, but you will be deprived of the rights of mankind. Your fellow creatures will shun you like an impure being; and even those who believe in your innocence will abandon you, lest they should be shunned in their turn. Go in peace! I have given you your life, but it is an existence worse than death." [129]

De Tocqueville's analysis referred to an America still almost entirely rural. Two generations were still to pass before big industry would even begin to dominate the American scene. Therefore we may conclude that the main features of popular totalitarianism also emerge prior to industrialism, in a way roughly parallel to the appearance of the major traits of centralized despotisms in pre-industrial times. Although the Geneva of Calvin's day showed us how sham democracy and mutual repression could work for a short while and on a small scale when reenforced by a central apparatus of terror, the "tyranny of the majority" is much further along the road toward popular totalitarianism, on a scale large enough to affect millions, not hundreds, of individuals.

Where modern industry on a grand scale has established itself firmly, conditions emerge that are much more favorable for popular totalitarianism. The familiar arguments pointing to the consequences of modern technology come into play here. Mass production, leading to a uniform style of life, reenforced by propaganda, advertising, mass entertainment, and the changes in the technology of warfare create, as many writers have pointed out, a totalitarian situation even in formally democratic states. As a rule, these factors are used to explain the rise of centralized totalitarian dictatorship in the twentieth century. Though these factors were significant in the emergence of the Nazi and Stalinist dictatorships, it is also possible that this form of repressive society may now be obsolete, at least in the technologically advanced countries.

What could conceivably take its place is a much more highly developed form of the tyranny of the majority. What would be the chief characteristics of such a society? Its most striking feature would be a change in the definition and dimensions of human autonomy and freedom. The citizen in such a state would believe that he was "spontaneously" and "freely" making the "right" decisions in all aspects of his life. But in reality both governed and governers would be caught in the same silken web of oversimplified alternatives, the "best" of which would be equally discernible to everyone, pounded home by efficient mass communications. In such a society all the members could be depended upon to repress each other in nonviolent ways so successfully that the central government could reduce its political functions substantially in favor of administrative maintenance of the new "best of all possible worlds." Crude police terror would be unnecessary. "Free elections" could continue since they would not constitute a threat to the established system.

With a high standard of living, popular demands for a different world might evaporate into a diffuse feeling of boredom, easily narcotized through minor changes in the plots of television shows. Professional intellectuals would no longer form the focal point for revolutionary social change but could be seduced by the material satisfactions of well-paid technical jobs. In any case, the need for a high degree of specialization in all intellectual fields could in time efface the memory of earlier standards and ideals with which to criticize the existing order. Social science could continue in the present direction until it eliminated all reasoned reflection about society. In the ultimate limiting case nearly everyone would be "reasonably" happy and would wash each other's brains to the point where the state at last could wither away.

Some sardonic readers may think that this sketch is no fantasy but a description of current reality. Leaving aside the important question of whether this is a true description of either a real or a potential society, a more serious critic might raise the following objections. All human societies, it might be argued, require devices to coordinate the activities of a number of individuals. In the past these devices have ranged from brute force through religion, law, and custom, to intimate face-to-face persuasion. Presumably something on this order will be necessary in any future society. To call all such devices brain washing in some imaginary future society, where people would admittedly be "happy," free of disease, terror, and overwork, the critic might conclude, is merely to fall victim to romantic and nihilist illusions. In short, the critic might ask, what is wrong with such a society?

The critic's query deserves an answer. But it raises issues that transcend by far the limits of this essay. To agree on what is wrong with such a society we would have to agree on a system of values, the meaning of happiness, and be able to distinguish between the discipline necessary to maintain an advanced industrial society and that which endangers human freedom. These issues go to the heart of contemporary social science and permeate the whole climate of serious thinking on modern society. Therefore we may pause to examine this climate, returning to these themes in the last two essays of this volume.

· 3 ·

THE NEW SCHOLASTICISM
AND THE STUDY OF POLITICS

It seems to be impossible to make any set of connected assertions about human behavior without taking a position on two questions. One of these is the relative weight to be given to empirical fact-gathering and to formal deductive logic, the elaboration of analytical categories and their relationship to one another. The other question concerns the moral position of the scientist in relation to his subject matter, a question that does not arise except in the study of human beings. Opinions here range from a thoroughgoing relativism and ethical neutrality to an equally straightforward moral absolutism, though there can, of course, be numerous varieties of the latter position. In the major writings on human affairs that pretend to scientific status, however, one can usually discern in any given writer an emphasis in the direction of two answers out of the four that are possible in taking a stand on these two questions. For the sake of convenience, we may call these emphases empiricism, ethical relativism, deductive formalism, and moral absolutism. I shall try to assess the advantages and limitations of these viewpoints, concentrating mainly on the last two that now arouse considerable interest among social scientists. To make the discussion more concrete, I shall comment in some detail on two recently published books, Marion J. Levy, Jr., *The Structure of Society*,[1] an example of the deductive-formalist tradition, and Paul Kecskemeti, *Meaning, Communication, and Value*,[2] a work that stops just short of a thoroughgoing moral absolutism. Any such classification is of course partly arbitrary. Through its crude mesh many important points will escape. If it brings others to the surface, it will have served its purpose and can be discarded.

The combination of emphases that has prevailed rather widely in the fairly recent past is a stress on the empirical and deductive tradition, along with the claim of complete ethical neutrality. Sumner's *Folkways* is a good example. The major assumption of this combination is that man is a part of nature and can be profitably studied, with modifications tailored to the subject matter, by the same means as the rest of nature. Essentially, the procedure involves the collection and classification of facts, and their ordering by appropriate hypotheses into a coherent logical scheme, subject to modification by further hypotheses. Deduction and formal logical treatment is therefore by no means entirely ruled out of court. But it is subject to considerable distrust, to be checked at every possible point by reference to empirical observation. According to this view, grand deductive schemes definitely should not be the starting point of concrete research. Scientific growth from this standpoint resembles the action of a spider spinning a web. The scientist may allow several strands of inference to wave in the wind, but until they attach themselves securely to facts that set the pattern for the web, he will be wary about trusting himself to the structure.

Throughout the investigation the scientist studying human beings is supposed to maintain the same detachment from his material as, let us say, the biologist dissecting a worm. His conclusions should not tell us what he wishes to discover, but only what he actually did discover. That this is a counsel of perfection all adherents of this view recognize clearly. At the same time, they would point to what they regard as substantial achievements gained in this fashion. The study of politics has been poorer in such achievements beyond the level of straightforward description than have other fields in the social sciences, for reasons that cannot be examined here. Nevertheless, many pages from the writings of Mosca, Michels, and some of Lasswell's earlier works, might be advanced by the empiricists and ethical relativists as examples of what can be done from this standpoint.

Those who hold this view seldom push their ethical neutrality to the point of asserting that social science has nothing to do with human welfare. Ordinarily they merely claim that ethical and political predilections have no place in the process of scientific inquiry as such. But they usually hold that the results of this inquiry will somehow be beneficial to mankind. In its more naive and superficial form, the empirical-neutral position frequently embodies the following diagnosis of our time: what is wrong with the world today is that the skills of the natural scientists have outrun those of the social scientists, as the latest bomb supposedly "proves." What is necessary, therefore, is for the social sciences to copy the natural sciences and overtake them. As soon as man has adequate knowledge of himself, he will be the master of his own fate.

The criticism of this diagnosis is at least moderately familiar and need not delay us long. Without being guided by some purposes and values that transcend such a narrow and technical view of disciplined inquiry into human affairs, it is argued, correctly I believe, that social scientists will rapidly become mere technicians selling their skills to any unscrupulous power-seekers who want to manipulate society for their own ends. I would be more disturbed about this problem if I were convinced that the social scientists already had in their hands powerful intellectual tools that could do the damage that is sometimes feared. So far we don't seem to know enough to be very dangerous.

Another variety of technical degeneration in the empiricist-relativist tradition may be more serious. The view is fairly widespread that the only problems that can be studied in a disciplined and scientific fashion are those that can be made to yield quantitative and measurable results. Its adherents therefore seek to break all problems into units for which quantification is — or at least superficially seems — appropriate. The rationale is that by getting positive answers to a series of small problems we will wake up some fine day with a conclusive answer to the big problems. This hope can be a realistic one only so long as some connection between the little problems and the big ones is kept clearly in mind. When this connection disappears in the search for easy problems with conclusive answers, the result is merely the piling up of disconnected trivialities.

There is also a certain pseudo-certainty about figures that exercises a dangerous fascination for Americans. Very crude and questionable facts are often submitted to overrefined and precise statistical manipulation. Not long ago a younger social scientist said to me that the best guarantee of scientific objectivity was a test of statistical significance. Such a position seems almost incredible. Tests for statistical significance indicate whether or not numerical findings on a large number of cases might be the result of chance. The meaning of "chance" results cannot be the same for any kind of investigation, and indeed in some types of research the concept of chance may be totally inapplicable.[3] There are grounds, discussed in the following essay, for holding that the logic of sampling does not apply to major problems of historical causation. Many who use tests of statistical significance and similar instruments in the search for objectivity have only a dim awareness of the reasoning behind their use.

The basic source of this overemphasis on technique seems to lie in the belief that it is possible to find technical routines and machines that will do *all* of our thinking for us. Instead of using old-fashioned and arduous methods of appraising the evidence, one can invent a piece of statistical litmus paper. Now, within limits, this viewpoint is quite correct. Technique can extend our powers of observation enormously, and aid us in uncovering errors in logic, while at the same time it opens up new areas of investigation. But technique alone cannot define what is scientifically worth investigating. Larger problems of the social milieu and, ultimately, of philosophy enter into any defensible judgment of scientifically significant problems. Ill at ease in such questions, many technicians search for pseudo-security in a form of pseudo-precision.

This search for pseudo-security seems to me to be on the increase among the younger generation of scholars, now in their graduate school apprenticeship. Harassed by financial and family worries, they are anxious to learn a technique that is just mysterious enough so that a businessman or government administrator won't quite know what to make of it. In this way they can acquire a professional label and get on with the task of making a living. The diffusion of the simpler stereotypes and the intellectual small change from the empiricist and rationalist tradition among influential sections of the lay population also encourages this trend. The practical businessman, the college president, and the foundation head readily give financial and administrative support to "projects" with a heavy emphasis on narrow technical results under the rationalization that some day it will "pay off" in greater understanding and welfare. These sociological factors reenforce the intellectual ones to produce the possibility that the social sciences may sterilize themselves. Fortunately, competing intellectual traditions and social forces may prevent such an outcome.

Among these competing traditions is the one I have provisionally labeled moral absolutism, which displays numerous signs of a revival, partly as a reaction to the more extreme technicism that has grown up within the empiricist and relativist position. Absolutism is in a way an unfair label to pin on the writers I have in mind. The simple word "moralist" would be better if it did not carry an overtone of preachiness. The position taken is not absolutist in the sense of dogmatic intellectual rigidity. Rather it is one of seeking with an open mind a well worked-out moral position as a standpoint for appraising human behavior generally and political behavior in particular, without giving up the attempt at explanation. Those who hold this position do not regard the task of disciplined inquiry as finished when the scientist has explained things as they are or have been. Instead, they also display a systematic interest in human affairs as they might be.

The moralist position has long been a strong one in political science and the source of jibes from those in neighboring disciplines who have believed in the essential neutrality of science. Since the war, however, there have been signs of movement toward the moralist position in the other disciplines. It has extended even into anthropology, hitherto the source of attacks on almost any moral position as a form of "culture bound," ethical provincialism and "ethnocentrism." I suspect that the change has a good deal to do with the discovery that the relativist and objective position leads to the conclusion that the social practices of Nazi Germany and Communist Russia cannot be condemned any more than cross-cousin marriage and the couvade. Some have stuck to their relativist guns and accepted the conclusion. Others have apparently been shocked into the search for a new intellectual position that would both explain these phenomena and provide a basis for negative appraisal. Much, though by no means all, of the postwar work by anthropologists on values, cultural themes, and national character owes its impetus, I think, to this recent experience. For several generations anthropologists have been interested in the variety of moral beliefs and practices exhibited by human beings and have sought to explain them within one or another strictly naturalistic framework. For that matter, very few serious scholars have ever argued that values do not belong to science, in the sense that they could not be the subject matter of detached scientific investigation. What is new is the idea that the scientist can have something to say about values and moral preferences that goes beyond a naturalistic explanation of their origin and relationship to other aspects of social behavior.

Since the actual and potential weaknesses of the search for moral absolutes have become familiar through the relativist critique, little need be said here. There is always the danger of confusing one's own historically limited moral climate with some universal principle that is somehow felt to be necessary for all of humanity at all times. There is also, to my mind at least, a tendency among many writers interested in this problem to become overly preoccupied with the philosophical implications of a particular doctrine and to neglect whatever relationship it may possess to the way people actually live, with the consequence that the stuff of human behavior becomes lost in a cloud of empty abstractions.

Like the search for valid ethical appraisals, the use of formal deductive methods in the study of social behavior has a venerable and respectable intellectual history. The recent return to a quasi-scholastic formalism is also partly a negative reaction to certain extremes in the empiricist tradition, particularly its older assumption that facts, once gathered, would somehow tell their own story. The story, so the deductive criticism runs, is always imposed upon the "facts" by the implicit or explicit analytical categories and hypotheses used by the investigator. Therefore, it is better to make these categories and hypotheses as explicit and logically watertight as possible at the outset of the inquiry, in order to force the data to yield a clear-cut decision in respect to the tenability of the theory. This doctrine has gained considerable force in recent years, to the point where the old-fashioned naturalist, the scientist who is chiefly a "good observer" of social behavior, has a difficult time in justifying his scientific status. A theory that is derived from careful examination of a body of facts is liable to be dismissed with the epithet of mere *ad hoc* explanation.

The pursuit of this doctrine to the exclusion of other considerations also leads to its own special form of exaggeration, exemplified in certain aspects of the work of Talcott Parsons and some of his students. It characterizes much of the volume by Marion J. Levy, Jr., *The Structure of Society*. I shall comment on this work in somewhat more detail shortly, but wish to set out first what seem to me some of the general difficulties inherent in this emphasis. As indicated by the appearance of Harold D. Lasswell and Abraham Kaplan's *Power and Society* in 1950,[4] Talcott Parsons' *The Social System* in 1951,[5] and Morton A. Kaplan's *System and Process in International Politics* in 1957,[6] this neo-scholasticism is no isolated phenomenon but represents a major intellectual trend among those professionally concerned with the study of human behavior.

In the first place, the development of abstract categories evidently has a seductive attraction in its own right, whether or not they are useful in ordering data. Though the formalists assert that the ultimate purpose of the development of categories is the manipulation of data, their assertion strikes me as being mostly a pious hope.[7] The actual procedure is primarily one of splitting verbal hairs with an axe. What emerges from the undertaking is a collection of verbal categories, empty file drawers, as it were, that are arranged in a neat and, at first glance, imposing pattern. All that remains, supposedly, is to fill some of the file drawers with facts, and the others will spring open with predictions. This would be quite true, and a tremendous achievement, if the relationship between the file drawers actually existed in the facts of social behavior. To permit valid inferences from one body of facts to another is the goal of any scientific theory. But in the case of the neo-scholastics, I submit, the relationship does not derive from the objective materials examined, but for the most part from the verbal symbols alone. And, for that matter, very few propositions, on the order of "if A is true, then B is also true," have come out of these reflections. In the Lasswell and Kaplan study there are a few, but they are usually so broad as to be quite meaningless. Opening this book at random I read, "PROP: Ruling practices are limited by the social order"; and "PROP: The rulers alter the regime whenever conformity to it is expected by them to constitute a significant deprivation." [8]

The second one I don't think is true, and the first one can mean anything. In Parsons' work, despite the richly suggestive paragraphs that are scattered in many parts of the study, there are fewer propositions, or hypotheses as such, than in Lasswell and Kaplan.

Even though a very high proportion of the formalists' work remains so far little more than a verbal juggling act, certain aspects of this approach have at least potential value. The emphasis on theory can serve as a healthy corrective to the mere accumulation of observations, without any reflection on their import. Furthermore, a system of categories or, more likely, fragments from such a system can frequently suggest new ways of looking at factual raw materials and become the source of hypotheses, even if they are not hypotheses themselves. While the great systems of the past now seem desolate intellectual ruins, important fragments from them are incorporated into what one may hope is a growing and at least partly cumulative intellectual tradition. Finally, it is certainly necessary to attempt the organization of conclusions derived from limited observations, scattered insights, and hunches into a more coherent whole that may often serve as a springboard for fruitful inquiry. It may even be argued that a set of verbal symbols can display some power to generate further symbols and ideas, as in mathematics, that eventually find their counterpart in the world of observable social behavior. Some such rationale seems to be behind much of the work now being done within the framework of the formalist and deductive tradition. At the same time, I believe that much more attention could and should be paid to the ways in which this counterpart is to be discovered, as well as to the question of whether the aspects of social behavior to be explained in this fashion are significant on other grounds. Almost any concept can be "illustrated" somehow or other, and facts picked up off the table and put into pigeonholes. This activity does not necessarily represent scientific progress.

II

In sociology the main version of the formalist tradition has become widely known under the name of structural-functional analysis. Marion J. Levy, Jr., gives one of the best recent expositions of this view in *The Structure of Society*. In a somewhat simplified and slightly inaccurate translation this form of analysis requires asking two types of questions about any set of social institutions that is being examined. The first question is: what activities must take place if this social system is to continue to exist? Such a question can be asked about an army, a monastery, a club, or a whole society, such as the United States. The other question is: how must these activities be carried on? For an army engaged in combat, part of the answer to the first question is that it must carry on the activity of killing the enemy, and part of the answer to the second question is that in order to do this it must have a certain type of command structure, a certain organization of supplies, etc. In this manner, one establishes the so-called functional imperatives of a certain type of social system.

As Levy stresses over and over again, the identification of these functional imperatives does not yet tell us anything about the life expectancy of the institution under analysis. Marxists and others have declared that the structural-functional approach is incapable of handling problems of change, because it merely tells us what is necessary for the maintenance of a particular type of status quo.[9] Levy regards this charge as unfounded. The establishment of the conditions necessary for the maintenance of a system implies neither an interest in its survival, nor an assertion that it will continue. The necessary conditions, i.e., the imperatives, may not be met, for a wide variety of reasons. History, as Levy remarks, is full of the wreckage of social systems that could not meet the requisites for their continuation. He maintains, however, as do others in this tradition, that to determine the necessary conditions of a particular set of social arrangements can be one of the most powerful first steps toward indicating the sources of internal strain in an institution and the lines of potential change.

After endeavoring to establish the validity of the functional approach, this school proceeds by an attempt to draw up a list of the imperatives, first for any type of society, and then for specific types of society. Though the procedure rapidly gets into terminological complexities that need not to be pursued here, the endeavor is often suggestive. Where it goes astray, I think, is in seeking too high a level of generality. As Levy admits, it is impossible so far to point to any kind of concrete social arrangement that is demonstrably necessary for *any* kind of social system. Likewise, I am very skeptical of Talcott Parsons' attempt to classify all forms of human action as necessarily falling under one of five pairs of alternative forms. There are perhaps a few illuminating

statements that can be made about *any* kind of human behavior, but most of them are likely to be banal. There is also
some usefulness in an effort to encompass the whole spectrum of social and political behavior in one intellectual *tour
de force,* as it were, with the aim of locating specific manifestations at their appropriate points on the spectrum. This
is perhaps the strongest argument that can be made for the
very high level of generality and abstraction that characterizes much of the structural-functional discourse. Until it
can prove its utility on much more concrete materials, where
only fragments of the scheme are likely to be applicable,
the over-all system will continue to resemble a theology
more than a system of scientific discourse.

At the level of specific contributions to the understanding
of politics, one aspect of the structural-functional scheme
has been helpful in assessing the significance of personality
factors in politics. Studies of "culture and personality" or of
"national character" have attracted considerable attention in
recent years. Parsons,[10] however, points out that social systems, of which an army may again serve as a useful example,
require people to behave in certain regular and predictable
ways that clearly have nothing to do with either individual
personality or culture. The relationships of command and
obedience and the hierarchy of authority show many similarities in the Spartan and American armies that can
scarcely be attributed to the personalities of the individuals
concerned, or to the nature of contemporary American or
ancient Greek culture. But they are readily understandable
in terms of what armies have to do and the way people
have to be organized to carry on these activities.

Personality and cultural factors, along with others, may on the other hand be absolutely necessary in explaining why a particular individual or group of people refuses to adapt to the imperatives of a specific social system or situation. Hitler's behavior certainly cannot be entirely explained in terms of the pressures upon him generated either in German society or in the larger system of world politics.

In general, social scientists are not quite sure whether the terms culture, society, and personality merely represent different ways of looking at the same body of facts, or whether, despite a vague area of overlap, they draw attention to phenomena that are genuinely distinct. Troubled by this state of confusion, Levy pleads for more precise usage of these terms and sets forth at length the bases for his analytical differentiation of society and culture.[11] While the terminology itself is an insignificant issue, I think he underemphasizes the partial autonomy of various fields of human behavior loosely covered by these terms. For example, in language, an area of culture that has been subject to the most precise and formal treatment so far, certain types of linguistic change can to a great extent be accounted for without reference to society or personality.[12] Phenomena displaying a similar degree of autonomy can probably be found in the development of the human personality.

III

Meaning, Communication, and Value, by Paul Kecskemeti, is also largely formal and deductive. But where Levy adheres to the tradition that science is neutral in ethical questions, Kecskemeti's problem is simultaneously a scientific and moral one. Recognizing that some adherence to a common set of values is a necessary basis for any form of group life, he asks whether rational consensus is possible among human beings on any grounds other than strictly scientific ones. Though I am not prepared to say that his affirmative answer carries conviction beyond any possibility of doubt, the steps through which he reaches it constitute in many respects a very thought-provoking treatment of a question with vital contemporary political implications. It also challenges a wide variety of received doctrines in nearly every field of social science.

Kecskemeti's major conclusion is that it is possible to make meaningful statements about values — that is, statements whose acceptance or rejection is not an arbitrary matter — dependent upon nonrational factors such as instinct and suggestion. His conclusion rests heavily upon a particular definition of meaning: "The meaning of an object A consists in determining which response is 'good' (or 'bad') in the situation in which A is present. 'Good' and 'bad' are taken here in the most general sense possible; any standard by which the result of a response may be judged satisfactory may define meanings" (p. 5). This definition leads him to the position, familiar in some German writings around the turn of the century, that the sciences dealing with the study of man cannot maintain a completely detached neutrality toward their subject matter. Since the organism puts certain demands upon its environment, the scientist in order to understand the meaning of the organism's behavior must apply, to some extent, the same standards as the organism itself. This argument does not imply that the scientist must accept the same standards himself; one need not be anti-Semitic in order to understand Hitler. It does imply that the search for completely value-neutral categories in the explanation of human behavior, as in some forms of experimental psychology, is unlikely to be very profitable. Kecskemeti rejects the possibility of explaining human behavior purely in terms of automatic responses to situations, as for that matter do many psychologists, and argues that complete prediction of human behavior is not feasible in principle (p. 120). Free of determinist bias, his intellectual system permits much greater freedom for fruitful reflection on what can be achieved in concrete political circumstances.

Since group life cannot be ordered by empirical science alone, he argues in one of his most telling passages, the confinement of rational discussion to strictly demonstrable scientific matters implies either a forced consensus in the totalitarian manner, or else a willingness to permit each individual to go his own way arbitrarily, to the destruction of all social life. The way out of this dilemma, the author proposes, is a systematic ordering of the manners of discourse that are appropriate to different types of values. Values he defines not according to the usual usage of something considered desirable, but as a method of ranking possible goals or objects of desire in terms of possible conflicts among these desires. Thus "decency" is not something desirable in itself. It is, as he puts it, a basis for preferring one way of behaving over another. The key to the argument is the following: those who discuss the "higher" values, such as truth, beauty, justice, and the like, accept certain postulates that provide a framework for subsequent discourse. Though the rejection of the postulate cannot be shown to involve either a logical contradiction or a factual error, the rejection itself has the "stringent consequence" that the rejecters can no longer participate in the type of social situation that the standard defines.

A tough-minded realist might argue on two grounds that Kecskemeti's solution is no solution at all. First, it merely pushes the point of arbitrary and undebatable assumptions back one step further, to the value postulates. Secondly, the exclusion from the social situation that the standard defines is unrealistic. Did Stalin ever count himself out of an argument about beauty or science or truth because he rejected certain postulates that the rest of the scientific or artistic community accepted?

IV

Most philosophers today would be likely to agree that it is impossible to construct a system of values, or to find a rational basis for criticizing and evaluating society and human behavior, without at some point making arbitrary assumptions. In closing I should like to point to some arguments indicating that it may be possible to do this after all.[13] If one who is not a professional philosopher ventures into an area where angels are wary, perhaps he may be forgiven since the philosophers have not yet given answers that the social scientist can use. To speak more sharply, most of the traditional philosophical answers look silly to an informed social scientist, who easily sees in them the rationalizations of a particular class and epoch.

And we need the answers badly. A rigidly factual approach soon runs up against the outer limits of empirical thought and has to cry for help.[14] Take the problem of the criteria for a free or unfree society, posed at the end of the previous essay. Do we take a man's word for it when he tells us that he feels free? Would we take a drug addict's word for it when he tells us that he is really happy? Common experience tells us that there are illusions and that we need some criterion to be on our guard against them and criticize them. How do we find these criteria?

We find them through science, if we define science broadly as disciplined and rational thinking. Science starts from observations but, by a process of reflection, open to verification at every step, it gradually reaches objective criteria for judging the facts. It does this, as Morris Cohen points out, by discovering the rational framework that underlies the external world. Some philosophers prefer to locate reason strictly in the human mind. That at once opens the door to mysticism and delusion.

In geometry, for example, man can reach the concept of the perfect circle through abstraction and definition. From very rough approximations in nature, such as the end of a log, he gradually works his way to the ideal concept. The perfect circle may not exist anywhere in nature, a problem we can return to in a moment. Yet the concept as such not only provides a method for understanding certain phenomena, such as a wheel, that approach a perfect circle, but also for evaluating these phenomena. In this way thought starts from the facts, but is able, as it were, to make the facts turn back on themselves in critical evaluation. It can do this through strictly secular methods. As I see it, such is basically the conclusion Hegel offers us at the end of his contradictions, when they are stripped of their mystical and quasi-religious overtones.

The human mind of course plays an active part in this process. That in itself is not important, so long as each step along the way is subject to verification, and free of arbitrary judgments as it moves along the line from facts to appraisals. As far as I can see, this is actually the case, though the history of failures in attempts to argue this position certainly warrants caution. The perfect circle, it must be admitted, does have a puzzling status for those with a strongly empirical turn of mind. If one limits the term facts strictly to sense data, the perfect circle does not exist at all. There is no need, however, to limit the notion of reality in this fashion. The perfect circle is just as real as any sense datum. Plato would of course have us believe it is more real. Morris Cohen argues that such concepts, including the basic idea of reason itself, are real in the sense that they constitute the basic structural framework that underlies the universe. The concept of a perfect society can perhaps be reached in the same way, taking off from real societies, to reach a critical standard. To create such a concept would of course be a tremendous undertaking. Perhaps the best we can do at any given moment in history is to draw out the potentialities of the social forms that exist before us in such a way as to set up a critical standard for evaluating the status quo.

A Kantian might object that any scientist's decision as to what constitutes a fact already involves certain prior decisions. For instance, the scientist uses such concepts as space and time, or nowadays space-time, in telling us what his facts are. Since these concepts are logically prior to the facts, in the Kantian view the scientist does not start from the facts at all. It does not seem to me that this objection is valid. The scientist by manipulating his data and reflecting about it reaches knowledge about these concepts in the same manner as he reaches other forms of knowledge. Finding the logical structure of the universe is an act of discovery. We cannot impose this order by an act of the will, though we may make provisional assumptions about it as we go along. Nevertheless these assumptions are subject to correction and verification as knowledge advances.

To the extent that the above arguments are correct it is in principle possible for social theory to get beyond empirical statement about the connections among social facts and reach tenable positions for evaluating society without turning into some form of dogmatic mysticism. Despite its abstract and somewhat philosophical character, the neo-scholastic tradition in contemporary social science shows practically no interest in social criticism. Social science has not always taken this position. As I shall try to show in the next essay, by trying to avoid political commitment, it can inhibit further advance in actual knowledge about society.

In making this point I do not intend to imply that all social theory must ultimately be some form of social criticism. There is a tremendous amount of valuable work to be done simply by way of discovering and establishing determinate relationships among the facts of social institutions and individual behavior. There is even a limited case to be made for the role of idle curiosity in social science, as well as in natural science. But if social science drops the task of rational criticism from its program altogether, leaving it entirely to theology, journalism, and the Bohemian fringe of intellectual life, it can some day drown in a sea of verbiage, strewn with floating bits of meaningless data.

· 4 ·

STRATEGY IN SOCIAL SCIENCE

The main evidence that a methodology
is worn out comes when progress within
it no longer deals with main issues.
Whitehead

To some persons the very notion of scientific strategy
seems contradictory. How can one conceive of a strategy for
discovering the unknown? Does not the discovery of new
knowledge always imply doing what one did not know
how to do before? Such persons stress the accidental nature
of past scientific discoveries. They are reluctant to criticize
any form of research, even that which at the moment seems
most futile and trivial, on the grounds that anything turned
up by human curiosity may some day contribute to one of
the great insights that mark a forward leap in human
knowledge.

There is some merit in this contention. Since we cannot
know in advance the fundamental discoveries of the future
we cannot decide with complete certainty whether any particular investigation is worthwhile or not. Nevertheless, the
intellectual and physical resources of both natural and social
science are limited at any one point in time. Cultural and
social factors also limit the direction of inquiry, emphasizing
some problems and pushing others into the background. In
other words, scientific strategy does differ from one society

to another and from one historical epoch to another. Whether we want to or not, we must have scientific strategies and must continually choose among them. A completely liberal policy of encouraging all sorts of inquiry on the grounds that a few may eventually succeed is therefore an utopian impossibility. In science, as in war, we are compelled to make estimates about promising and unpromising lines of attack. We can reduce the element of uncertainty in scientific strategies, but we can never eliminate it completely.

Aware, then, that the problem is unavoidable and the solution necessarily uncertain, let us begin with a backward glance at the strategy of social science in nineteenth-century society. Historians tell us that the society we designate loosely by the term nineteenth-century existed mainly in Western Europe and the United States between Napoleon's defeat and the outbreak of World War I. For our purpose we do not have to be precise about either the chronological or the geographical boundaries. We can start easily enough with de Tocqueville and end with Freud. Any selection is bound to be somewhat personal and arbitrary. The other men will therefore be mainly sociologists, though we may be allowed glimpses at other fields. No one would put Marx, Durkheim, Weber, and Mosca on exactly the same plane of intellectual attainment. Nevertheless nearly every one would agree that they had important things to say about human society. Even the casual reader will sense at once, I believe, a qualitative difference between these nineteenth-century thinkers and men widely regarded as leaders in the field of sociology today: Parsons, Merton, Stouffer, and Lazarsfeld. Without going very far into details, and therefore perhaps with some injustice to all concerned, let us try to put our finger on the nature of this difference.

It is legitimate, I think, to regard our nineteenth-century writers as participants in a single debate about the possibility of putting into practice the principles proclaimed earlier by the French Revolution. To be more precise, they were arguing about the feasibility of creating a rational society under the conditions of industrial advance and with the human materials available at that time. For them "rational" had a definite social content and implied, even if loosely, the kind of society that would enable man to make the most of his creative capacities. None of them, not even Marx, were naive utopians. All of them saw in their own way that mankind had destructive capacities as well as creative ones. But they also cast about in terms of their own discoveries and insights to find ways of taming, limiting, or eliminating these destructive forces.

There was a strong historical current in the thinking of all these men. Through different lenses and from widely differing political standpoints all of them saw as their scientific problems those which the course of human history had put on the agenda as the significant ones of their epoch. Since these problems are still very much with us, it may be helpful in assessing our own strategies to recall very briefly some of the ways in which these nineteenth-century figures viewed them.

Leaning slightly toward the conservative viewpoint, Alexis de Tocqueville set out to discover what happened when a society transplanted from Europe and freed from some of the incubus of European conditions and traditions tried to realize the ideals of the French Revolution. Though he found much to admire in America, he was disturbed by a certain uniformity of tone in American life, that derived, he thought, from the absence of social contrasts, and especially the absence of any class that was the carrier of an aristocratic tradition. As noted elsewhere in these essays, he was apparently the first to perceive clearly the possible dangers of a system of mass democracy, a theme that became more and more prominent in nineteenth-century social thought.

Mosca, also, to continue the conservative argument, found his original intellectual stimulus in the French Revolution. Influenced by Taine's critique, he set out to criticize some of the humanitarian ideals that had accompanied the Revolution and were an important part of his intellectual climate as well as ours. Though Mosca's theories shade over at times toward fascism, his thinking still remained within the framework of liberal thought. His ideal society was English parliamentary democracy of the nineteenth century, which he recognized as actually an oligarchy with benevolent traits. Though he set out to demonstrate, in opposition to Aristotle, that all governments are in practice oligarchies, he recognized important differences among them. To my mind his most important contribution was to put social and historical content into older legalist ideas about the division of powers in the state. Like de Tocqueville he recognized that liberty under law required, if it were to mean anything in practice, a situation of conflicting and competing interest groups in society such that no one class or group could completely dominate the state. For the same reason he distrusted social doctrines that pretended to have all the answers. "When power rests," he said, "on a system of ideas and beliefs outside of which it is felt there can be neither truth nor justice, it is almost impossible that its acts should be debated and moderated in practice." [1] Writing long before the advent of modern totalitarian regimes, he was one of those who foresaw this possibility as a consequence of the decline of a property-owning middle class and the rise of secular schemes of salvation.

Among the radicals, Marx, the "bad conscience of the bourgeoisie," is, of course, the main figure. Today we try to quiet this bad conscience by saying that Marx was more a moralist than a scientist. Insofar as he was a scientist, so the argument against him continues, he may have called attention to some of the uglier features of nineteenth-century capitalism (though he has been accused of overdoing these as well),[2] which modern capitalism has subsequently overcome. His basic notion, the opponents claim further, that one could discover "laws of motion" from history and the study of contemporary society, represents an illegitimate transfer of antiquated notions from physical science into the study of human affairs. From these considerations the conclusion emerges that enlightened modern intellectuals can afford to treat Marx as an antiquarian curiosity.

To discuss these issues would take a book in itself. We must confine ourselves to one or two sketchy remarks. Few serious thinkers today would deny that Marx is antiquated in important respects. Even those sympathetic to Marx are likely to concede, for example, that there is little factual basis now for the hope that the proletariat will revolt and destroy the repressive features of modern capitalism. After these and other concessions have been made to Marx's opponents, what remains is, to my way of thinking, still very impressive. The conception of social class as arising out of an historically specific set of economic relationships and of the class struggle as the basic stuff of politics, constitute some of the most important ideas that students of history and political behavior carry around in their heads, whether they are Marxists or not. As for the characteristics of capitalism, certainly the modern American version is something very different from that envisaged by Marx. Nevertheless I doubt very much that one can either understand the nature of this transition or analyze the present situation without drawing very heavily on Marxist ideas. The trend toward monopoly is, after all, an inherent part of the Marxist analytical scheme. As for the present situation, there can be no doubt that for a whole generation now the stimulus of war industry has played a vital part in maintaining American capitalism as a going concern. To put the point squarely, we have not had for some time the kind of capitalism that cured its own "faults," either through intelligent public policy, or through some automatic economic mechanism — if indeed such an animal ever existed. Whether we have learned enough to do this now, and whether the future will give us the opportunity to put this knowledge into practice, are questions to which we can have no certain answer.

One crucial aspect of Marx's strategy as a social scientist remains to be mentioned. More than any of the other writers considered here he started from the conviction that the social institutions of his day were evil. With his somewhat optimistic historical view, he believed that this evil was both transitory and unnecessary. At the same time he thought of himself as a scientist — a savage one to be sure, constantly using hard facts to strip away the veil of hypocrisy and unconscious self-deception that concealed the ugly realities underneath. For Marx there was no conflict between his position as a moralist and a scientist. The whole enterprise of science made sense for him only in terms of moral convictions. On this score Marx differs entirely from the dominant spirit in contemporary social science. Furthermore, Marx took it for granted that in any society there was a sharp divergence between the values and aspirations expressed in a society and the way the society actually worked. He would have been the last one to deduce social institutions from values, a line of thought that is prominent today. Perhaps he went too far in the opposite direction. Nevertheless, puzzled surprise at the gap between ideals and reality, as expressed in this professional review of a book on class in American society, is foreign to Marx's thought:

The facts, so far as they are known, about stratification in the United States are well introduced by Kahl's book. It remains to be found out why the dominant American ideologies tend to deny them. In spite of vast differences in economic privilege, the dominant creed holds this to be a classless society. In spite of the vast differences in power between the citizens and between their organizations, this is visualized as a democratic society in which everybody shares equal powers. . . . It is indeed baffling that statements about society in the major ideologies of the time and the land bear such little relation to the factual structure of sociey.[3]

The main conservative themes in serious nineteenth-century thinking about society occur in de Tocqueville and Mosca, the main radical ones in Marx. Are there, then, neutrals among the men mentioned above? If we designate as neutral any theory that has no significant political implications, it becomes very difficult to pin this label on any of these writers as long as we look at their work as a whole. Freud, as every one knows, fought a long uphill struggle against social taboos that prevented men and women from acknowledging even the existence of the facts he discovered about humanity. In this respect his discoveries are revolutionary and critical. On the other hand, his work to some extent justified the restraints laid by Western civilization on instinct and impulse. One could call Freud a neutral only by saying that these two trends in his thinking cancel each other out, a dubious and not very illuminating statement. As a man who was extremely skeptical about the possibilities of a rational society — a skepticism he expressed very clearly in *Civilization and Its Discontents* — we might best be justified by placing him in the conservative tradition. Where we place him is vastly less important than realizing both the conservative and revolutionary implications of his work.

Weber and Durkheim are the two that modern thinkers would be most inclined to classify as neutrals, at least at first glance. There are certain trends in the thought of these men that lead toward the superficially neutral stance of modern social science, as well as some of its other traits that strike me as very dubious. We shall come to these points shortly. But there is good evidence against labeling them neutrals.

To be sure, Max Weber said some very pungent and

worthwhile things against using the academic lecture platform to inoculate students with the teacher's personal philosophy. These remarks may reflect his fundamental decency and political courage. To my knowledge he never implied either in word or deed that social science should withdraw from burning political issues, though he did feel that there were limits to what science, strictly conceived, could contribute to their solution.[4] From time to time he was savagely critical of reactionary forces in German society,[5] and also of what he regarded as pseudo-democratic wishful thinking about modern industrial society.

Toward the close of a long essay on the possibilities of middle-class democracy in Russia, published shortly after the 1905 revolution in that country, Weber expressed very pessimistic and critical views, that make interesting and disturbing reading a half century later.

It is highly ridiculous to ascribe to advanced capitalism, as it is now being imported into Russia and as it exists in America — this "inevitable stage" of our economic growth — any real affinity for democracy or even with freedom (in *any* sense whatever of the word). Rather, the only real way to put the question is: How are any of these things possible at all in the long run under its rule? . . .

We individualists and partisans of democratic institutions are against the stream of material events. He who wants to be the standard bearer of a "developmental tendency" should abandon these old-fashioned ideals as soon as possible. . . . It is in the large continental areas, of North America on the one hand and of Russia on the other, whose monotonous plains favor schematization, that the center of gravity . . . of Western culture is moving forward unceasingly, as it once did in late classical times. . . .

"Correct" Social Democracy drills the masses in the mental goose-step and directs them toward a Paradise in this world instead of toward an otherworldly one (which in Puritanism certainly had respectable achievements to show in the interest of freedom in this world). In this way it makes a sort of vaccine that serves the interests of the existing social order.[6]

Similar ideas continue to find expression along the maverick fringe of social science today. But generally times have changed. Naturally Weber was no man to parade the pageant of a bleeding heart before the public. At the same time he had no fear of the sacred cows in his society. Can one really imagine today a president of the American Sociological Society as the author of a biting history of General Motors, or a penetrating attack on the political philosophy of the CIO?

Durkheim may come a little closer to deserving the title of neutral, though on balance he seems to me to belong with the critical conservatives. Yet at least two of his major works, *Suicide* and the *Division of Labor,* may legitimately be read as muted indictments of the modern world. The concept of anomie is part of a long tradition with overtones of romanticism that stresses the heartless mechanical nature of modern society. The same theme runs through the *Division of Labor*. His standpoint also, be it noted, remains historical. He uses the facts of suicide to illuminate modern society as a whole against a broad historical canvas, doing his best to connect forms of suicide with the stages and epochs of human history. The reason we might call Durkheim a conservative is because very little that society at any point requires of the individual can from his standpoint be a proper subject of rational criticism.

The last observation leads us toward the trends in the thought of these two men that culminate in some of the less fortunate assumptions of contemporary social science. There are virtues in these defects. In Durkheim and Weber the virtues perhaps still outweigh the defects.

One trait, particularly noticeable in Durkheim, is the positivist desire to base theory on facts and on facts alone. This strategy at times implies choosing smaller problems for the sake of firmer results, as Durkheim did in *Suicide*. Despite the loose edges of uncertainty that do remain, a modern reader is likely to feel real intellectual pleasure at watching Durkheim demolish one fuzzy hypothesis after another with an array of carefully chosen facts, to emerge with a theory of his own that fits the facts available to him. Here at last, one begins to feel, sociology is getting its feet firmly on the ground.

On further reading and reflection some of this sense of satisfaction may disappear. The positivist commitment begins to produce some odd results as early as Durkheim. Respect for the facts tends to become an inhibition on criticizing the facts, though Durkheim's historical perspective saves him from a complete acceptance of whatever exists.

His difficulties become apparent as he tries to develop an empirical method of making value judgments by taking over from medicine the distinction between the normal and the pathological. As he develops his case, he first concludes that whatever social facts are common are normal and that the unusual ones are the pathological ones. "Nous appelerons normaux les faits qui présentent les formes les plus générales et nous donnerons aux autres le nom de morbides ou de pathologiques." [7] This view would, of course, commit one to an acceptance of the status quo as "normal." A few pages further on he modifies this criterion very seriously, pointing out that social facts may be an adaptation to circumstances that are historically obsolete. Then he goes on to note that a social fact may be very widespread and still have no more than the appearance of normality.[8] As the historical perspective declines in later sociological thinking, so too does the capacity to analyze critically the existing social order. Sociology runs the risk of being left with only the first half of Durkheim's formula.

The decline of the historical perspective is already visible in the later works of Max Weber, particularly in *Wirtschaft und Gesellschaft,* the first part of which is available in English under the title of *The Theory of Social and Economic Organization.*[9] Here Weber was trying to conceptualize the enormous mass of historical material at his command. Though the classification remains illuminating where it brings out actual connections between real facts, as in the discussion of types of political systems and their relation to forms of economic life, a large part of the work is an arid desert of definitions. Here begins the tradition of abstract formalism in sociology. After Weber, Simmel carries it further, trying to abstract from social life the elementary and invariant forms, such as domination, subordination, and many others. The tradition would seem to have developed about as far as it could in the work of Leopold von Wiese.[10] After that, however, the tradition passed to the United States, where Talcott Parsons has elaborated it further. Now it constitutes the main body of sociological doctrine in this country. Since we have already discussed some of the main features of the formalist tradition in the preceding essay, there is no need to examine them further at this point.

Instead we are ready to attempt an answer to the earlier question: what is the main difference between the older strategy in social science and the prevailing one? When we set the dominant body of current thinking against important figures in the nineteenth century, the following differences emerge. First of all, the critical spirit has all but disappeared. Second, modern sociology, and perhaps to a lesser extent also modern political science, economics, and psychology, are ahistorical. Third, modern social science tends to be abstract and formal. In research, social science today displays considerable technical virtuosity. But this virtuosity has been gained at the expense of content. Modern sociology has less to say about society than it did fifty years ago.

The difference "jumps in your eyes," as the French say, if we compare the opening sentences of important statements on a significant problem, the nature of social classes, in a few of the authors mentioned: Marx, Weber, and Parsons. The contrast in what authors choose to put first in their discussions can scarcely be accidental. Any one who knows the three authors reasonably well would agree, I think, that these three passages do not misrepresent the character of their thought.

Let us begin with the famous discussion of the class struggle as it opens in the *Communist Manifesto:*

> The history of all hitherto existing society is the history of class struggles.

Freeman and slave, patrician and plebeian, lord and serf, guild-master and journeyman, in a word oppressor and oppressed, stood in constant opposition to one another, carried on uninterrupted, now hidden, now open fight, a fight that each time ended either in a revolutionary reconstitution of society at large, or in the common ruin of the contending classes.[11]

This sweeping generalization can be read mainly as a factual assertion, though an evaluative element enters in through the use of the words "oppressor" and "oppressed." But to Marx, at any rate, the facts would, as we have seen, make no sense without this evaluative element. He certainly was willing here and on other occasions to talk about the "facts" of oppression, struggle among social classes, and historical change. Indeed, Marx puts them first of all in this discussion.

They have not disappeared in Weber though he begins more formally with a definition:

The term 'class status' will be applied to the typical probability that a given state of (a) provision with goods, (b) external conditions of life, and (c) subjective satisfaction or frustration will be possessed by an individual or a group. These probabilities define class status in so far as they are dependent on the kind and extent of control or lack of it which the individual has over goods or services and existing possibilities of their exploitation for the attainment of income or receipts within a given economic order.[12]

The unequal character of class still appears in Weber's first sentence, which is obviously saying something about concrete societies. On the other hand, it is static and ahistorical in comparison with Marx. Compare Talcott Parsons:

It has come to be widely recognized in the sociological field that social stratification is a generalized aspect of the structure of all social systems, and that the system of stratification is intimately linked to the level and type of integration of the system as a system.

The major point of reference both for the judgment of the generality of the importance of stratification, and for its analysis as a phenomenon, is to be found in the nature of the frame of reference in terms of which we analyze social action.[13]

From these sentences the process of abstraction, to be discussed in the next section, has eliminated all reference to political struggles, oppression, and historical change.

They have retreated into the background of most academic thinking about society.

II

Let us now examine the ideal social science sets up for itself. What do its leading practitioners think it ought to be? What are the characteristics of the intellectual structure they are trying to create? Here again I shall speak mainly of sociology with an occasional glance at other social sciences.

As physical science moved away from the mechanical determinism of the nineteenth century, social science tended to abandon the corresponding grand syntheses of historical determinism to the point where the latter are now generally in very bad repute. In their place there has grown up a body of deductive theory, widely referred to as structural-functionalism. The key idea in this body of theory, the reader may recall, is the view that for every society there exists a certain limited number of necessary activities or "functions," such as obtaining food, training the next generation, etc., and an equally limited number of "structures," or ways in which society can be organized to perform these functions. Essentially, structural-functional theory searches for the basic elements of human society, abstracted from time and place, together with rules for combining these elements. It gives the impression of looking for something in human society to correspond to the periodic table of elements in chemistry.[14]

The ultimate objective in this line of thinking is the establishment of abstract quasi-mathematical formulae about human society from which it should be possible to derive the particulars of human behavior in any specified situation. Or to put the point in another fashion, the proponents of this view hope to subsume more and more individual facts that now appear as isolated observations about society in a single logically coherent structure. This viewpoint corresponds very closely with the natural science ideal of being able to reduce all phenomena to a series of related propositions.[15] The fundamental statements in this structure are expected to be universal propositions or scientific law. Let us see to what extent social science has succeeded in this goal of imitating natural science.

Natural scientists seek in the main two kinds of universal propositions. One takes the form of a static correlation, asserting that when A occurs B also occurs, as when we say that water freezes at 32 degrees Fahrenheit. Ordinarily natural scientists try to go beyond a mere static correlation to explain why the relationship holds. The other kind of proposition takes the form of a mathematical function,* asserting that X varies as Y does, as in the relation between pressure and volume in a gas. Again some kind of an explanation is given. While scientific explanations are tied together as firmly as possible, ultimately they take the form of descriptive propositions.

When we compare this model with the actual performance of social science, the contrast is striking. As even those most enthusiastically committed to the model will admit in candid moments,[16] social science, after some two hundred years, has not yet discovered any universal propositions comparable in scope or intellectual significance to those in the natural sciences. The situation does vary, of course, from one discipline to another. Sociology, as one of my colleagues is fond of remarking, constitutes from this standpoint the science with the hollow frontier, since it lacks any core of established theory, or any framework of general propositions strong enough to convince a substantial part of the profession.[17] Psychology is perhaps somewhat better off. Pavlov and those who have followed in his footsteps have established through laboratory methods a fairly large body of propositions. However, their significance in explaining more than a tiny segment of human behavior remains very doubtful. Though the explanatory power of Freudian theory is much greater — perhaps even too great — its scientific status is less secure. Classical economics managed to erect at one time a comprehensive and elegant theory to

---

* It should perhaps be pointed out that the mathematical concept of function is not identical with the sociological one.

organize its subject matter in a scientific manner. Somehow the facts have changed since the formulation of the theory. It may be significant that one of the leading figures in the tradition of classical economics, Professor Frank H. Knight, is also one of the most sharp-tongued opponents of a literal-minded transfer of natural science methods into the study of human affairs.[18] Whatever the variety among the different disciplines, it is safe to assert that the generalizations of social science nowhere approach the range and cogency of those in physics or chemistry.

The fact that we do not yet have any laws in social science comparable to those in the natural sciences does not by itself prove that such laws will never be discovered. Nevertheless it justifies raising once more the question whether social science is on the right track in making the search for such laws its chief *raison d'être*. The differences between natural science and social science may concern more than the relative crudity of social science. The logical structure of the kinds of knowledge we seek in social science may not be identical with that in the advanced natural sciences. It may be profitable to consider this possibility through examining the relationship between abstraction and additions to knowledge.

Natural science and social science both make use of abstraction from the raw data of experience in order to frame concepts and theories. Nevertheless the procedures of abstraction vary from one field of knowledge to another in accord with the nature of the materials studied and the purpose of the inquiry. In many fields, perhaps all of them, there is a certain tension between the desire to do justice to all the facts and the need to frame a logically coherent and esthetically satisfying theory. There is in other words a tension, perhaps an irreducible one, between particulars and universals.

Abstraction is not an end in itself. Indeed the end or purpose for which the scientist makes abstractions and seeks propositions lies, to some extent, outside the realm of empirical science. Even strict positivists now recognize this point. Philipp Frank has recently asserted that the validation of scientific theories "cannot be separated neatly from the values which the scientist accepts." [19] Therefore any system of abstraction that omits facts which the investigator wants to understand is automatically inadequate. There are then strong grounds for suspecting that we have so few universal propositions in the social sciences because such propositions frequently do not give us the kind of knowledge we really seek.

In human affairs the mere fact of uniformity or regularity, expressible in the form of a scientific law, may often be quite trivial. To know that Americans drive on the right hand side of the street is to know something that permits predictions about American behavior and meets all the formal requirements of a generalizing science. Such knowledge does not, however, meet the criterion of significance. The same comment applies to many generalizations that social scientists seek with a technical apparatus and logical rigor that contrasts ludicrously with the results. Here is a recent example. From a study of "Male Sex Aggression on a University Campus" we learn that:

Of the 291 responding girls 55.7 per cent reported themselves offended at least once during the academic year at some level of erotic intimacy. The experiences of being offended were not altogether associated with trivial situations as shown by the fact that 20.9 per cent were offended by forceful attempts at intercourse and 6.2 per cent by "aggressively forceful attempts at sex intercourse in the course of which menacing threats or coercive infliction of physical pain were employed." . . . A 3×3 table yielding a Chi square significant at the .05 level suggests that episodes of lesser offensiveness are concentrated in the fall and more offensive episodes in the spring.[20]

The professional journals are full of similar articles where careful methodology is used on trivial problems. Unfortunately most of them are not as amusing as this one. If the demonstration of uniformities like these were all that social science had to offer, it would constitute no more than an enormous diversion from more important problems.

Uniformities in social behavior become significant for us only when they concern important problems, such as freedom and compulsion. What is important is not a matter of subjective whim, but is the consequence of a specific historical situation. The important regularities in human behavior, as well as some of the trivial ones, are found within the context of historical change. For example, one can observe recurring patterns in the behavior of a slave-holder and still other patterns in those of a feudal lord. There may even be some common features in all the major historical forms of domination. To find them would be a worthwhile task, and in an earlier essay I have suggested possible common features in the "natural history" of systems of domination. But we certainly cannot stop there, even if we arrive at such a point. Accurate knowledge requires that we understand each social type, slave-holder, feudal lord, capitalist entrepreneur, and socialist bureaucrat, within its proper historical context, that is, in relation to previous forms and possible subsequent ones.

Above all we must not make the mistake of thinking that some universal necessity inheres in social relationships that are limited to a particular historical epoch, such as capitalism or, for that matter, socialism. To abstract from all historical situations in the hope of discovering some pan-human or universal kind of social necessity does not seem to me a very promising procedure. Can we really make any worthwhile generalizations that apply equally well to the Stone Age and to twentieth-century America?[21] Perhaps one cannot answer this question with a flat negative in advance, though I remain most skeptical. One certainly has the right to object vehemently to any science that eliminates from its vision all change that has taken place between the Stone Age and the twentieth century merely for the sake of formulating universal propositions like those in the natural sciences.

Let us look more closely at some of the procedures modern social science theorists use when they try to arrive at universal propositions. As noted earlier, these scholars often tend to abstract from the reality of historical trends in order to concentrate on resemblances and differences in the hope of formulating scientific laws. For them, history, if it is used at all, becomes merely a storehouse of samples. Using historical data, one can supposedly discover the social correlates of democracy, tyranny, class struggle or class peace,[22] and the like. The existing body of theory should, from this standpoint, indicate the likelihood or unlikelihood of finding a particular combination of traits. Historical and social facts are then drawn upon as if they were colored balls from an urn, and the results subjected to tests for statistical significance in order to disprove the hypothesis or derive additional support for it.

The trouble with this procedure is that it starts with the assumption that the facts of history are separate and discrete units. This assumption is basic to statistical analysis. "The fundamental notion in statistical theory," says an advanced theoretical text, "is that of the group or *aggregate,* a concept for which statisticians use a special word — population. This term will be generally employed to denote any *collection of objects* under consideration, whether animate or inanimate. The notion common to all these things is that of aggregation." [23] The modern social scientist searches for invariant laws that govern the relationship among these atomized observations reflected in statistics. Such laws are implicitly or explicitly thought to apply to masses of single facts of equal importance, which are expected to display at least the statistical regularity that molecules do in a gas under specified conditions.

It is in this conception, I think, that the modern social scientist goes astray. Though I too would reject any thorough historical determinism, I do not believe that the significant facts of history are mere mechanical aggregates. Instead, they are connected with one another over time.

The point may be clearer if we refer to a concrete problem. Franz Neumann has pointed out how dictatorship has at certain times in history served to prepare the ground for democracy by breaking the resistance of privileged social classes.[24] This is a crucial point that helps us to understand dictatorship, class struggles, and democracy in a context of continuing historical growth. Now, such a point would necessarily be hidden from an investigator who proceeded by some widely used procedures in deductive social science. Dictatorship and democracy would be separated into airtight compartments with carefully worked out definitions of each. Then other facts would be sorted into neat piles labeled "dictatorship" and "democracy." The whole process by which one social structure passes into the other would become invisible. Such a procedure might, to be sure, uncover some important and unsuspected connections. One cannot reject it as totally useless. But the most significant problem would remain hidden.

I doubt very much that the logic of sampling is at all appropriate to historical problems of the type just mentioned, where the investigator is studying the change from one type of social structure to another. In sampling techniques, as shown by the familiar image of drawing balls from an urn, the researcher examines the numerical distribution of traits in the sample to make inferences about the universe from which they are drawn. His main problem is whether or not the sample is representative of the whole. The historian too looks at some of the facts in order to make inferences about the rest of the facts. He also, in other words, has to make a connection between the parts and the whole. But the historian's connection has a different form. The notion that he works with frequently is that of stages of historical development. Now any given stage of historical development is to some extent the product of a preceding stage and the source of subsequent stages. Even the most anti-determinist historian uses such a notion. This kind of connection is missing, as I see it, in the logic of sampling. In an atomized universe the numerical character of the sample does not "cause" the universe to have a corresponding numerical character, nor does it by itself affect the character of subsequent samples drawn from the same universe.

From a strictly logical standpoint one could avoid the preceding difficulties by including the concept of time as a specific variable, and working with some form of mathematical function. Historical writings often do have the logical form of a mathematical function, as when they assert that political changes have accompanied economic advance or economic decline. Perhaps even some of the Hegelian insights into revolutionary upheavals as the final result of slow cumulative structural change can be expressed in the form of discontinuous functions. Mathematics does not limit itself to the study of quantity, and cannot be excluded from any field of knowledge merely because the latter seeks knowledge that goes beyond quantitative relationships.[25]

Whether one can leap from such observations to the claim that mathematics can weave a web around *any* body of facts is a question I am not competent to answer. This claim does seem to imply potential omniscience in the manner of a Laplace, and therefore strict determinism, a position from which natural science has been retreating rather rapidly for some years. This question does not seem to be a very fruitful one to ask just now. We can easily afford to wait until a mathematical genius encompasses all history with his mathematical net, and decide then if it improves our understanding. In the meantime there is work to be done.

The real question then concerns the gains and losses involved in mathematical abstraction. Here again we cannot give a firm answer because we cannot know what discoveries in mathematics may come along that might some day constitute a powerful analytical tool. But we do know in a general way that we do not want our gains in logical rigor and ease of manipulation to be at the expense of too much historical content.

Nor can mathematical sophistication do much to help us out where our data are inadequate for other reasons. There is no use drawing intriguing curves and computing intricate functions on the basis of badly collected statistics. Such devices merely conceal the real problem. Good judgment on all these questions requires training on problems that lie outside mathematics as such. We can use the mathematical notion of function, but it will not do everything for us. Current overuse and misuse of statistics and abstract mathematical models in social science stem in my opinion partly from the failure to present fledgling students with other adequate criteria for distinguishing important truth from accurate triviality. For this reason it is not a problem that can be solved merely through the improvement of mathematical techniques.

Certain virtues in the mathematical way of thinking deserve explicit recognition here. The use of mathematics compels the investigator to state his propositions in an unambiguous manner that automatically permits a tight chain of deductions leading to a firm result. If the original premises are correct, and the chain of deductions made without error, the truth of the conclusion is guaranteed. The difficulty, on the other hand, is that at present the act of putting statements about society in the form of mathematical premises requires such simplification that the essential elements in the facts are likely to be lost or seriously distorted. The lack of ambiguity in the original propositions may therefore be spurious. The trouble here may lie as much in mathematics as in social science proper. So far, at any rate, the results have not been striking. As one of the most enthusiastic advocates of mathematical methods in the social sciences has observed recently, "Even the most ardent optimist would not claim that mathematics has yet led to important discoveries in the behavioral sciences." [26]

The decline of the historical perspective and the rise of a formalist deductive tradition in search of laws has been accompanied by an increasing static bias in much contemporary social science. For this there are several reasons. The search for categories that apply without reference to time or place easily introduces a static bias unless we are extremely careful to notice the historical limits of our generalizations. The very notion of a scientific law implies a relationship that holds whenever and wherever it occurs. Naturally if one could really demonstrate that any given law really held for human affairs, it would be nonsense to assert that formulating such a law and writing it down introduced a static bias into thinking about society. What often happens, however, is something else. The investigator discovers, or thinks he has discovered, a relationship that actually holds for a limited period of history, and extends it unjustifiably into the future. Most scholars are too cautious to make flat statements like this in print, and a clear example from recent writings does not come to mind readily. The bias is in the air more than in print. Not long ago social scientists used to say to one another in informal conversations that Soviet experience "proved" the need for inequalities of income, prestige, and authority in any form of industrial society.[27] Actually Soviet experience merely tends to demonstrate the necessity for such inequalities at a particular stage of industrial and technological growth. The Stalinist era also shows that totalitarian methods are effective for catching up rapidly with advanced industrial countries. Future technological progress, such as more advanced automation, may make possible very gross changes in the structure of authority, prestige, and inequality. If we looked at this problem with nothing but dubious laws in our heads about the "functional imperatives of industrial society," we could easily go astray. Though the notion of functional imperative has its uses and can lead to valuable insights, we must be careful to realize its limitations.

Closely related to the preceding difficulties are those derived from the importation of equilibrium theory into social science, which may also produce a static bias. In equilibrium theory the key assumption is that any social system tends toward a state of rest in which the conflicts and strains among its component parts are reduced to a minimum. Most people are aware that in real life this movement toward a state of rest may not actually take place. Some try to get around the difficulty by asserting that the equilibrium assumption is not one about empirical facts, but a purely theoretical assumption that serves to order the factual material into a consistent whole.[28] No one would object if this were the case, but it is difficult to see how the equilibrium viewpoint can account for certain fairly well established facts. For example, in the judgment of some historians, the attempts made by later Roman emperors to strengthen the empire contributed to the growth of feudalism, or, in other words, to the replacement of one social system by a quite different one. In technical language, meeting the "functional imperatives" of the system had destroyed one social system and led to its replacement by another. Again, in modern times the New Deal may be plausibly regarded as an attempt to shore up American capitalism. But the effort to do this led in turn to marked modifications of American society. Perhaps structural-functional theory could somehow account for these changes by saying that these efforts to restore equilibrium led to unanticipated and dysfunctional consequences. We may leave aside the question of what gain to real knowledge such statements bring. To my mind they amount to throwing the equilibrium assumption overboard by saying that tendencies toward equilibrium are unexpectedly producing change.

The Hegelian dialectic with its conception of developing contradictions that lead to intermittent abrupt changes provides, one may argue, a better heuristic guide to the explanation of many important processes of historical growth. In any case it would appear that the decision whether equilibrium theory applies or not is basically an empirical one, to be decided after careful study of the facts.

We come then to the conclusion that a static bias and

a tendency toward triviality pervades much contemporary social science quite largely, though not entirely, because of the model that it sets for itself in copying the successful procedures of the natural sciences. Other social factors play a part in this. They may even be the more important ones, though I have purposely left them aside to concentrate on the smaller problem of the way in which social science may limit itself through its own ideals. In closing this part of the discussion it may be worthwhile to mention briefly some of the social factors which favor the present direction of social science.

One factor may be that the United States, where the kind of social science just discussed flourishes best of all, is at the present juncture a prosperous country at a high point in its power. American society has some of the qualities of an *ancien régime,* though it is worthwhile remembering that the Soviet Union has a good many of these too. The critical spirit may not flourish just now because our social and economic problems are mild relative to those of other times and other places. Furthermore, the historical point of view is likely to remind us of the transitory nature of social institutions, generally an uncomfortable thought in an *ancien régime*.

At a more detailed level of analysis one may note that many modern social science research projects are very expensive affairs. They require the collaboration of a large number of persons with a variety of skills and training. Often their cost exceeds several hundred thousand dollars. It may be unfair to remark that the results are not always in proportion to the costs. But it is true that the present situation in social science is the exact reverse of what prevailed during the great theoretical discoveries in physics in the nineteenth and early twentieth centuries. Revolutionary advances were made with limited funds and, by modern standards, crude laboratory equipment. Today, in social science at any rate, the effect of large grants is to give to those in control of the allocation of research funds a highly strategic position for determining which problems will be investigated and which ones will not. It is also true, of course, that older systems of economic support for intellectuals, such as patronage and direct dependence on the market, exercised some influence over the ideas developed by professional intellectuals. The varying impact of all these factors is certainly not understood in any detail. But it is clear that in older times patronage and the market did not succeed in shutting off thought critical of the existing social order. Under the present situation the need to be a cooperative member of a research team may do more to stultify original and critical thinking than direct economic pressure. At the same time it is difficult to conceive of the foundation director who will readily allocate several hundred thousand dollars for a research project that is likely to come up with conclusions that reflect very seriously on important interest groups in the United States. The result is that creative thinking has to take place, if it can take place at all, mostly in the interstices between Big Theory and Big Research.

III

The importance of historical relationships has come up

repeatedly in the discussion so far. It is to the historian, therefore, that we may turn in search for a different approach to the problems of human society. The historian's approach too has its severe limitations. But first let us look at the way he pursues his craft.

The most fruitful historical research generally begins with an awareness of some problem that is felt to be significant. This importance may stem either from some major contemporary issue, a starting point that in my view arouses unnecessarily the suspicions of many professional historians, or some unresolved problem in explaining the sequence of human institutions. In the most successful cases the collection and interpretation of the facts is a one-man operation. Though historians emphasize, I believe correctly, the individual nature of creative thought, it would be unfair to overlook the services that are provided for them by large-scale bureaucratic organizations. I have yet to hear the most individualist scholar object to the advantages offered by a large and well-run library.

Though some famous historians have been men who have pursued an *idée fixe,* this type of work sooner or later runs into some of the disadvantages of overemphasis on logical deduction discussed in the preceding section. The best results emerge from the confrontation of the evidence with a wide variety of ideas, often contradictory ones, acquired in the course of broad reading and some experience of men and affairs. Sometimes the most important discoveries may occur as a consequence of the temporary block produced by an inconvenient fact which forces the investigator to abandon previously accepted explanations. Darwin too says somewhere that one can always learn most from facts that are exceptions to our theories.

The preceding methods the historian shares more or less with other students of society. There remains a very important difference between the way historians and modern quantitative social scientists treat their facts.

The quantitative social scientist, as we have seen, abstracts from his materials only those features that can readily be arranged in a numerical order. After running these features through a statistical sieve, he draws conclusions from the size of the different piles before him. The historian, on the other hand, usually examines each piece of potentially useful data carefully, turning it over and over in his hands in its raw state, as it were, to see what light it may shed on his problem. In this way the historian brings to bear on each new piece of information all the knowledge that he has acquired up to that point. The historian's knowledge grows while he is examining the individual facts. That of the quantitative social scientist comes only after a large number of facts have been sorted.

The famous Swiss historian Jacob Burckhardt describes the historian's approach succinctly in the introduction to his magnificent *History of Greek Culture*. Though the procedure lacks method in the superficial and mechanical sense of the word, the logical justification rests on the way it produces cumulative insight and knowledge. I quote directly from Burckhardt's German, since it has a personal flavor impossible to reproduce in translation:

Woher weiss [der Forscher] was konstant und charakteristisch, was eine Kraft gewesen ist und was nicht? Erst eine lange und vielseitige Lektüre kann es ihm kund tun, *einstweilen* wird er lange Zeit manches übersehen, was von durchgehender Wichtigkeit war, und einzelnes wieder für bedeutend und charakteristisch halten, was nur zufällig war. Bei der Lektüre ferner wird ihm, je nach Zeit und Stimmung, Frische und Ermüdung, und besonders je nach dem Reifepunkt, auf welchem sich seine Forschung gerade befindet, alles, was ihm gerade in die Hände fällt, unbedeutend und inhaltlos oder bezeichnend und interessant in jedem Worte erscheinen. Dies gleicht sich nur bei fortgesetztem Lesen in den verschiedenen Gattungen und Gegenden der griechischen Literatur aus; gerade mit heftiger Anstrengung ist hier das Resultat am wenigsten zu erzwingen: ein leises Aufhorchen bei gleichmässigem Fleiss führt weiter. . . .

Wir sind "unwissenschaftlich" und haben gar keine Methode, wenigstens nicht die der andern.*

The chief advantages of the historian's procedure are its flexibility and cumulative insight. Since the historian is also primarily interested in change, his image of social reality stresses growth, transformation, and decay. On these counts we may conclude that the historian is superior to the modern social scientist.

Nevertheless, when the historian faces the problem of

* "How does the scholar come to know what is constant and characteristic, what has been a force and what has not? Only prolonged and wide reading can reveal this to him. *Meanwhile* for a long time he will overlook many things that were of general importance, and regard details that were merely incidental as significant and characteristic. In the course of further reading, everything that he comes across will strike him as either unimportant and meaningless or characteristic and interesting, in every word — according to the hour of day and his mood, his freshness or weariness, and especially according to the stage of maturity which his research has actually reached at that moment. All this evens itself out only through continued reading in the various genres and areas of Greek literature; least of all can one force the result through violent effort: a gentle and attentive listening, with the effort evenly applied, carries one further ahead. . . . We are 'unscientific' and have no method at all, at least not that of the others." Jacob Burckhardt, *Griechische Kulturgeschichte* (Kröners Taschenausgabe; Stuttgart, 1948), I, 7–8. Italics in original.

making his knowledge capable of explaining more than particular historical facts, he often fails miserably. He is generally unwilling or unable to transfer the knowledge gained from understanding one set of social relationships, say the history of modern Germany, to another set, say modern France. The professional equipment and predilections of the historian make him unfit for such a task. (We shall try in a moment to answer the question whether this is a reasonable task to impose on a historian or, for that matter, on anybody.) When the historian is pressed to make his information useful in a practical way, such as by presenting an estimate of future trends in some part of the world with which he is familiar, he frequently responds in one of the following ways. First of all, he may simply refuse, saying rather smugly, "History must not be confused with prophecy." If pressed still further, he may make a guess on the basis of a single crude parallel, predicting for example, the future of Russia on the basis of events following the French Revolution. Most frequently of all he will retreat from such pressures into literary snobbishness and pseudo-cultivation. This takes the form of airy generalizations about the way history provides "wisdom" or "real understanding." Phrases to this effect often occur toward the end of historians' reviews of other historians' books in media for the general public, like the *New York Times*. Anyone who wants to know how this wisdom can be effectively used, amplified, and corrected will find that his questions usually elicit no more than irritation.

Thus the historian, as a rule, is unwilling to proceed beyond intuitive hints to a form of knowledge that approaches science in becoming a set of explicit propositions that can be tested and corrected. What is the reason for this situation? Social scientists today generally make the following diagnosis of their own difficulties, and include the historian merely as an extreme case. The principal difficulty, they assert, in obtaining transferable knowledge or valid generalization lies in the inadequacy of our contemporary conceptual schemes. Here, therefore, is the front on which the main attack should be directed. Natural science, according to this view, had the same difficulty in its early stages. Scientists overcame it by learning new ways of thinking about their subject matter.[29]

The social scientists are mistaken, I believe, in making the difficulty only a subjective one of getting the right ideas into our heads. Actually the problem is a rather subtle one involving both the character of the materials we study and the things we want to learn about them. If knowledge in any field of inquiry is to be transferable, the material itself must display certain uniformities and regularities. We cannot force this regularity on the material through sheer intellectual agility. These uniformities may not only be absent; they may also be, in terms of important human values, the less significant aspects of the subject matter we study. Where such uniformities are either absent or constitute for us the less significant aspects of the material, we gain nothing by trying to force the subject matter into a framework of scientific generalizations.

The latter situation prevails rather widely in the study of human society. As H. Rickert, the main proponent of this thesis, points out, we are not interested in the qualities

Goethe shared with other human beings, such as the fact that he had two eyes, two arms, and two legs. Goethe is not a lump of coal, whose only interest to us is the qualities it shares with other lumps of coal and whose properties can be expressed in the form of scientific generalizations. What we want to know and understand about Goethe is his unique contribution to human civilization. To some extent we can acquire this understanding only by uncovering a unique pattern of connections between unique events.[30] The usual argument against Rickert's thesis holds that we only understand the unique to the extent that we can analyze it into elements that are not unique. Certainly this is one way in which the advance of knowledge proceeds. But it is not, to my mind, the only way. We can readily perceive the connection between a series of historical events, even though what is important to us in these events cannot be placed in a category with other events. This argument holds even for studying large-scale historical units, encompassing more than one society, such as royal absolutism, parliamentary democracy, totalitarianism.

Essentially Rickert's argument comes down to saying that it is unfair to ask the historian for knowledge that is generalizable, while it is nevertheless possible for the historian to give us, in principle at least, rigorous and unambiguous factual answers to important questions. Some significant questions do not require and indeed do not permit answers in the form of a scientific generalization.

Though this is not the whole story, it is worthwhile pursuing this line of thought further and examining its consequences. Two antithetical positions can emerge and have emerged from this radical historicism. One is a nihilistic and self-defeating pedantry that wishes to study history for its own sake. Its one redeeming virtue is that it seeks to eliminate from our view of the past the distortion that arises from an excessive effort to perceive our own difficulties in earlier stages of civilization, such as the mechanical projection of contemporary problems onto the waning Roman Empire. Though I do not think that the sole function of scholarship is utilitarian, yet why should we put our best energies into studying the past, or for that matter the present, if the results cannot serve somehow as a guide amid our own perplexities and anxieties?

The other position is an exaggerated form of voluntaristic optimism, which denies that the past exerts any determining force on the present. Karl Popper, the philosopher, seems to me to represent an extreme version of this doctrine. If history is not subject to any laws of development, the implication follows that man is free to control his own destiny. To my way of thinking this optimism too is demonstrably shallow. Throughout human history nearly all human beings have been confronted with the overwhelming weight of a society they as individuals did nothing to create. They have lived out their lives within a very narrow range of alternatives. Only a few gifted persons have had the opportunity and the ability to break through the barriers of their time and place.

The historical approach to human affairs, it appears, finally runs out into absurdities and trivialities as it is pushed without reflection toward its logical conclusion. So too, I have tried to argue, does social science in the image of mathematics and natural science. At this point we seem to have reached a dead end. If one rejects both the major positions discussed in this paper, what is left? Now it is one of the conventions of current discussion that a writer must end his paper with constructive and positive suggestions. It is tempting to break with this convention and write: *Finis*.

IV

However, man's struggle to understand himself and his world continues, and has no small successes to its credit. In what follows I can do no more than outline in a sketchy manner what seems to me a promising strategy for the future.

First of all, there is no blinking the fact that in the study of human affairs we are often confronted with the need to comprehend the unique. At the same time there is no reason to be especially agitated about this situation. In many other areas of life men orient themselves to reality by learning its unique features. The navigator, for instance, depends on charts that show the location of individual reefs and shoals. The same virtue inheres in first-rate descriptions of current social institutions, especially where they are sufficiently grounded in history to permit rough estimates of the dynamics of the situation. Here we simply have to reconcile ourselves to the probability that much research will never be cumulative in the sense that research is cumulative in the physical sciences. Social facts do not display the same degree of repetitive uniformity as do those of inorganic nature. To concentrate on what repetitive uniformities there are in social facts is to lose sight of their most important characteristic, growth and change over time.

As we look more closely at chains of historical causation and the way they are treated by reflective historians, we may realize that there is still another way of resolving, at least partially, the tension between the particular and the general. Those who have come either directly or indirectly under the influence of Hegel see the general as manifested *in* the particular or the unique. Thus, Marx saw the general features of mid-nineteenth-century capitalism, as it had developed out of earlier social forms, in the single case of nineteenth-century England. England was at that time the most advanced form of a capitalist economy. On the basis of an understanding of the inherent dynamic characteristics of competitive capitalism, he tried to predict the form it might take in the future. He made mistakes, as any man can do with any method. This does not prove that the method itself is unsound any more than mistakes in arithmetic count against the science of mathematics. Many other historians perceive, or think they perceive, the general culmination of an historical trend in a particular event. Thus an historian studying the decline of the Roman Republic may easily say in effect, "By this time the situation had developed to the point where Caesar took the decisive step and crossed the Rubicon."

In using this procedure the historian tries to perceive the general in the atypical or even the unique, resolving in this fashion the tension between universals and particulars. Perhaps this way of putting the point gives it too much of a deductive and scholastic air. What actually happens, at least in many cases, is that a unique fact or event enables the historian to choose between two or more interpretations that have been building up in his mind on the basis of materials he has been examining up to then. It is clear that this procedure is not limited to the historian's craft or the analysis of past events. We use it on those that are happening currently. For example, whenever a significant new piece of information becomes available about the Soviet Union some hypotheses are proved wrong and others proved correct. To pursue this example further, when a major figure is dropped from the Soviet leadership, some hypotheses about the nature of significant political processes in that country (not merely intrigues at the top) can often be confirmed or disproved. As the Marxist philosopher, Karl Korsch, pointed out some twenty years ago, this procedure is similar to that of the crucial experiment in natural science.[31]

There are important differences, however. In the natural sciences, researchers are able to repeat their experiments, an advantage that social science lacks for its most important problems. Furthermore, within limits, the actions people take in important historical crises can alter the nature of the situation. Before General Zhukov was removed from the Party Presidium in 1957, the hypothesis that the army was gaining power might have been just as correct as the hypothesis that the Party had control of the situation. (Actually, of course, we don't know.) His removal resolved the ambiguity, at least for the time being. Thus a particular historical event can do more than confirm or disprove a hypothesis. It can change the situation so that one hypothesis or another *becomes* correct. There would seem to be an irreducible element of indeterminancy here, roughly similar to that in modern physics.

Nevertheless it is very difficult to believe seriously that the sequence of historical events is purely random, or that anything can happen at any time. The range of possible variation would seem to be markedly reduced when we consider the sequence of major institutional structures, such as the transition from the Roman Republic to the Empire. There is in human affairs an area of freedom, but it is limited. What the limits are at any one point of time, including the present, has to be determined in large measure through empirical investigation. Social scientists sometimes feel themselves to be second-class citizens in the scientific community because they cannot make as firm predictions as their colleagues. There is no need for this if they define their task as making accurate assessments of the limits and possibilities of effective human behavior. Such assessments make sense of course only in terms of some prior set of values. There is no reason for the social scientist to cut himself off from reasoned discourse on such questions when in fact he ought to have some of the most important things to say.

It is worthwhile drawing attention to further characteristics of this procedure and the way it differs from those used rather widely in the social sciences today. Seeing the general in the historically unique is a method of abstraction different from that of omitting more and more of the characteristics of what we are studying until the residue is something approaching pure form without content. The latter procedure is the one that the formalist tradition now follows in sociology. Furthermore, this way of seeking generality through history also differs from trying to understand a society by observing the social practices that are most common in it and that thereby supposedly "typify" the society. Instead the historical approach teaches us to try to "see the grass growing beneath the ground" or to find in atypical practices and beliefs the seeds of possible future developments. To be sure one often has to discover, often by statistical counting, what is typical before one knows what is atypical. But to do this is merely the first step in the analysis.

Social science, we may conclude, is therefore not precluded from finding principles of change that apply to more than a single series of events. It is here I believe that the great theoretical achievements of the future will some day come. They will, no doubt, come slowly and develop out of existing traditions, from Hegel to the evolutionary doctrines of the late nineteenth century. Some contributions from the formalist school and structural analysis may also find their proper place in a larger synthesis. Let us see if we can discern, even if very dimly, what some of these ideas might be.

When we say that something changes, we usually mean that there is also some constant feature, which enables us to see that we still have before us the original object. What constant element can we legitimately point to in the study of human society? The concept of social evolution, though under a cloud today, provides an answer to this question. Social evolution is a process that remains essentially the same while continually producing new results.

When the concept of social evolution came to the fore in

nineteenth-century sociology, mainly through the influence of Herbert Spencer, it became entangled with a number of other notions that served to discredit it. These notions do not, however, constitute essential elements in the concept and can be discarded without damage to the valid core.

One of these entanglements was the notion of unilinear development. Sooner or later, according to this view, all societies pass through the same stages of social development.[32] Clearly this theory will not stand up and has been effectively disposed of by Boas and others. It is more accurate to think of evolution as a series of related processes leading to very different consequences.

Even though no society passes through *all* the stages, the concept of stages in social evolution is still a valuable one. It can be applied to specific aspects of society and culture, such as economic structure and technology. From this standpoint one could construct a chronological series of major types of economic institutions from primitive hunting down to the large-scale modern bureaucratic firm.

Certain societies, it would then appear, have been the major vehicles or concrete manifestations of each stage. Furthermore, as Hegel and Marx recognized in their different ways, each society that constituted a specific stage of social development carried the process of growth in a particular direction about as far as it could. Then the society fell victim to limitations produced by its own success, as the level of adjustment, crystallized into social institutions, prevented further advance. Human societies often come to resemble middle-aged tennis players who continue to rely on a second-rate serve learned long ago. After the process of growth has ceased, due to vested interests and other causes in one society, another previously backward society may carry it forward again.

I am not altogether convinced by the Marxist argument that changes in the way men produce and exchange material goods constitute the main propelling force in this process of change. New ideas may also play an equally important role. Perhaps the two are inseparable. Was not the steam engine originally an idea? This point I do not propose to discuss further. There is nevertheless a strong tendency, which Marx recognized, for the various institutions and beliefs in any society to hang together in at least a roughly coherent fashion. Modern structural-functional theory has caught sight of the same fact and elaborated it, while attempting to rip it out of the evolutionary and historical context. Along with this tendency for social institutions to adjust to one another, at a particular stage of social development — what Sumner called the strain toward consistency — we must recognize the continual disruption that occurs in particular societies through the skipping of historical stages. The modern Orient, where the most advanced technology jostles ancient social institutions, such as caste, constitutes a familiar example of stage-skipping.

Another cardinal point in nineteenth-century evolutionary doctrine concerns survivals. Here we enter territory where it is more difficult to separate the wheat from the chaff. At first, anthropologists thought they saw societies which they called primitive "living fossils" of early stages of social history. These "living fossils" they then tried to arrange in an evolutionary series. This attempt largely failed. Anthropologists soon realized that their "primitives" or "living fossils" were actually our contemporaries and had behind them just as long a history as we do ourselves. Furthermore, in some respects, especially kinship, these societies were extremely complex, while modern society had become very simple. For these reasons anthropologists rejected the notion that these societies could serve as evidence about our social ancestry and shied away from the concept of social evolution. Such societies were simply to be regarded as different and equally valid forms of civilization, to be judged in their own terms. The word primitive disappeared from the anthropologists' vocabulary, not only on account of its evolutionary connotations but also because of its derogatory overtones. Even the term nonliterate replaced preliterate for similar reasons.

This relativist attitude, now on the wane, performed useful services in combatting some of the cruder ethnocentric prejudices in Western scholarship. Furthermore, the attempt to reconstruct an evolutionary series for nonliterate societies undoubtedly contained many dubious propositions. Nevertheless there are grounds for holding that this wholesale rejection was mistaken. If it is true that any society sooner or later falls victim to the limitations of its own success, cases of arrested development should be the rule rather than the exception. In areas of the world remote from the main centers of cultural innovation, societies might remain at roughly the same stage of advance for centuries. Nor does the presence of elaborate and complex kinship systems in many nonliterate societies contradict the principles of social evolution. Rather we should expect to see that in some parts of the world certain forms of social organization had been tried out, elaborated as far as possible, and then abandoned in the course of subsequent development. It is perfectly possible for kinship to reach a high degree of complexity while technology and economic and political institutions remain rudimentary. In biological evolution, too, the elaboration of one organ, while the rest of the organism remains simple, occurs very often. In man it is only the brain that is highly developed. No one, I suppose, would be inclined to classify a lobster as a more advanced form of life than *homo sapiens* because it can swim backwards faster than an Olympic backstroke champion.

Anthropologists now show some signs of modifying their anti-evolutionary position. Particularly in works addressed to the layman one may observe a stress on the historical growth of human society and culture. This stress marks a return to important evolutionary positions.[33]

If these comments serve at least to reduce the suspicions of those who remain hostile to the conceptions of social evolution, we may proceed to a few remarks about the process itself. In a work almost completely ignored by modern social science, A. G. Keller formulated the main principles in a fashion perhaps crude but basically correct and capable of refinement in the light of additional evidence. To reproduce the main points makes his views sound bald and abstract, a distortion that is nevertheless unavoidable. There are three: (1) Variations occur over time in the way a particular society solves the problem of adapting to its environment. (There are also, of course, variations among different societies in the way they solve their adaptive problems.) (2)

Selection takes place which favors the more successful adaptations. (3) The more successful adaptations are transmitted by social mechanisms to the next generation. Variation, selection, transmission — these are the heart of the continuing process by which mankind reaches ever new results.[34]

Several subprocesses, to which other writers have drawn attention, may be grouped conveniently under these main headings. Since this is scarcely the place to write a system of sociology, I shall do no more than draw attention to a few that strike me as especially important. First is the fact, already discussed, that a society's capacity for variation may and often does become limited after a spurt of innovating adjustment.[35] Second is the phenomenon of drift, to which Sapir called attention in his study of language.[36] Generalized out of its linguistic context, drift is the tendency of a society to change continuously over time in a particular direction on account of its structure.[37] There is obviously a fascinating field for research here, to which structural analysis, when freed of its present static limitations, may make important contributions. At the same time we must not overlook the point, also made by Hegel, that changes in society, as in nature, often take the form of qualitative leaps from one kind of structure to a totally different kind.[38] In other words, we must not be blinded by the mistaken dictum of Leibniz, *natura non facit saltus.* This leads us to the third point. Some processes of evolutionary change, such as the growth of scientific knowledge, are clearly cumulative. Others are much less so, or perhaps not cumulative at all. Cumulative growth is possible, it has been suggested, only where the nature of the social task permits specialization and cooperation through the division of labor.[39] In those areas of society and culture where change is less cumulative or even not cumulative at all, we may often discern, against a background of broader historical change, recurring patterns, as essentially the same institutional forms arise and decay in response to basically the same problems. This recurrence is particularly evident in political institutions, as I have tried to point out in the first essay in this book.[40]

The theory of social evolution, as is apparent from this discussion, cannot serve as a premise from which the social scientist might deduce the future with unfailing exactness. Such prediction on any really important scale probably is not feasible in the study of human society. The reason for this situation appears to be a matter of principle rather than a question of inadequate knowledge. Increases in knowledge about human society have contradictory results, similar to those expressed by the indeterminacy principle in physics. As we learn more about a political and economic situation in the attempt to forecast its outcome, the additions to our knowledge thereby change the situation and increase the number of possible ways in which it can turn out. Since Keynes's writings have become part of the common stock of economic wisdom, it is rather unlikely, even if other factors were alike, that a depression could run the course described in older economic texts. There may be some theoretical upper limit where the knowledge about the relevant factors in a situation catches up with the knowledge that changes the relevance of these factors. That happy day when social science bites its own tail is far enough away for us to ignore it now.

Social scientists, we may conclude, condemn themselves to unnecessary frustrations by trying to erect an intellectual structure that will permit predictions in the manner of the natural sciences. Meanwhile, preoccupied with its efforts to become "scientific," social science overlooks more important and pressing tasks. The main structural features of what society can be like in the next generation are already given by trends at work now. Humanity's freedom of maneuver lies within the framework created by its history. Social scientists and allied scholars could help to widen the area of choice by analyzing the historical trends that now limit it. They could show, impartially, honestly, and free from the special pleadings of governments and vested interests, the range of possible alternatives and the potentialities for effective action. Such has been, after all, the aim of inquiry into human affairs in free societies since the Greeks. One may still hope that the tradition can survive in modern society.

· 5 ·

THOUGHTS ON THE FUTURE
OF THE FAMILY

Ἄνθρωπος ἐὼν μή ποτε φάσῃς ὅ τι γίνεται αὔριον —
Simonides

Among social scientists today it is almost axiomatic that
the family is a universally necessary social institution and
will remain such through any foreseeable future. Changes in
its structure, to be sure, receive wide recognition. The major
theme, however, in the appraisal American sociologists
present is that the family is making up for lost economic
functions by providing better emotional service. One work
announces as its central thesis that "the family in historical
times has been, and at present is, in transition from an institution to a companionship." In the past, the authors explain,
the forces holding the family together were external, formal,
and authoritarian, such as law, public opinion, and the
authority of the father. Now, it is claimed, unity inheres in
the mutual affection and comradeship of its members.[1] Another recent work by a leading American sociologist makes
a similar point. The trend under industrialism, we are told,
does not constitute a decline of the family as such, but
mainly a decline of its importance in the performance of
economic functions. Meanwhile, the author tells us, the

family has become a more specialized agency for the performance of other functions, namely, the socialization of children and the stabilization of adult personalities. For this reason, the author continues, social arrangements corresponding rather closely to the modern family may be expected to remain with us indefinitely.[2]

In reading these and similar statements by American sociologists about other aspects of American society, I have the uncomfortable feeling that the authors, despite all their elaborate theories and technical research devices, are doing little more than projecting certain middle-class hopes and ideals onto a refractory reality. If they just looked a little more carefully at what was going on around them, I think they might come to different conclusions. This is, of course, a very difficult point to prove, though C. Wright Mills, in a brilliant essay, has shown how one area of American sociology, the study of crime, is suffused with such preconceptions.[3] While personal observations have some value, one can always argue that a single observer is biased. Here all I propose to do, therefore, is to raise certain questions about the current sociological assessment of the family on the basis of such evidence as has come my way rather casually. In addition, I should like to set this evidence in the framework of an intellectual tradition, represented, so far as the family is concerned, by Bertrand Russell's *Marriage and Morals,* that sees the family in an evolutionary perspective,[4] and raises the possibility that it may be an obsolete institution or become one before long. I would suggest then that conditions have arisen which, in many cases, prevent the family from performing the social and psychological functions ascribed to it by modern sociologists. The same conditions may also make it possible for the advanced industrial societies of the world to do away with the family and substitute other social arrangements that impose fewer unnecessary and painful restrictions on humanity. Whether or not society actually would take advantage of such an opportunity is, of course, another question.

It may be best to begin with one observation that is not in itself conclusive but at least opens the door to considering these possibilities. In discussions of the family, one frequently encounters the argument that Soviet experience demonstrates the necessity of this institution in modern society. The Soviets, so the argument runs, were compelled to adopt the family as a device to carry part of the burden of making Soviet citizens, especially after they perceived the undesirable consequences of savage homeless children, largely the outcome of the Civil War. This explanation is probably an accurate one as far as it goes. But it needs to be filled out by at least two further considerations that greatly reduce its force as a general argument. In the first place, the Soviets, I think, adopted their conservative policy toward the family *faute de mieux*. That is to say, with their very limited resources, and with other more pressing objectives, they had no genuine alternatives. Steel mills had to be built before crèches, or at least before crèches on a large enough scale to make any real difference in regard to child care. In the meantime the services of the family, and especially of grandma *(babushka)*, had to be called upon. In the second place, with the consolidation of the regime in the middle thirties, Soviet totalitarianism may have succeeded in capturing the family and subverting this institution to its own uses. At any rate the confidence and vigor with which the regime supported this institution from the early thirties onward suggests such an explanation. Thus the Soviet experience does not constitute by itself very strong evidence in favor of the "functional necessity" of the family.

If the Soviet case does not dispose of the possibility that the family may be obsolete, we may examine other considerations with greater confidence, and begin by widening our historical perspective. By now it is a familiar observation that the stricter Puritan ethics of productive work and productive sex have accomplished their historical purposes in the more advanced sections of the Western world. These developments have rendered other earlier elements of Western culture and society, such as slavery, quite obsolete, and constitute at least prima facie evidence for a similar argument concerning the family. Let us ask then to what extent may we regard the family as a repressive survival under the conditions of an advanced technology? And to what extent does the modern family perform the function of making human beings out of babies and small children either badly or not at all?

One of the most obviously obsolete features of the family is the obligation to give affection as a duty to a particular set of persons on account of the accident of birth. This is a true relic of barbarism. It is a survival from human prehistory, when kinship was the basic form of social organization. In early times it was expedient to organize the division of labor and affection in human society through real or imagined kinship bonds. As civilization became technically more advanced, there has been less and less of a tendency to allocate both labor and affection according to slots in a kinship system, and an increasing tendency to award them on the basis of the actual qualities and capacities that the individual possesses.

Popular consciousness is at least dimly aware of the barbaric nature of the duty of family affection and the pain it produces, as shown by the familiar remark, "You can choose your friends, but you can't choose your relatives." Even if partly concealed by ethical imperatives with the weight of age-old traditions, the strain is nevertheless real and visible. Children are often a burden to their parents. One absolutely un-Bohemian couple I know agreed in the privacy of their own home that if people ever talked to each other openly about the sufferings brought on by raising a family today, the birth rate would drop to zero. It is, of course, legitimate to wonder how widespread such sentiments are. But this couple is in no sense "abnormal." Furthermore, a revealing remark like this made to a friend is worth more as evidence than reams of scientific questionnaires subjected to elaborate statistical analyses. Again, how many young couples, harassed by the problems of getting started in life, have not wished that their parents could be quietly and cheaply taken care of in some institution for the aged? Such facts are readily accessible to anyone who listens to the conversations in his own home or among the neighbors.

The exploitation of socially sanctioned demands for gratitude, when the existing social situation no longer generates any genuine feeling of warmth, is a subtle and heavily tabooed result of this barbaric heritage. It is also one of the most painful. Perhaps no feeling is more excruciating than the feeling that we ought to love a person whom we actually detest. The Greek tragedians knew about the problem, but veiled it under religion and mythology, perhaps because the men and women of that time felt there was no escape. In the nineteenth century the theme again became a dominant one in European literature, but with the clear implication that the situation was unnecessary. Even these authors, Tolstoi, Samuel Butler, Strindberg, and Ibsen, in exposing the horrors and hypocrisies of family life, wove most of their stories around the marital relationship, where there is an element of free choice in the partner selected. Kafka's little gem, *Das Urteil,* is a significant exception. With magnificent insight into the tragedy on both sides, it treats the frustrations of a grown-up son forced to cherish a helpless but domineering father. Henry James' short story, *Europe,* is an effective treatment of the same relationship between a mother and her daughters. Despite some blind spots and limitations, the artists, it appears, have seen vital aspects of the family that have largely escaped the sociologists.

In addition to these obsolete and barbaric features one can point to certain trends in modern society that have sharply reduced rather than increased the effectiveness of the home as an agency for bringing up children. In former times the family was a visibly coherent economic unit, as well as the group that served to produce and raise legitimate children. The father had definite and visible economic tasks, before the household became separated from the place of work. When the children could see what he did, the father had a role to be copied and envied. The source and justification of his authority was clear. Internal conflicts had to be resolved. This is much less the case now.

It is reasonably plain that today's children are much less willing than those of pre-industrial society to take their parents as models for conduct. Today they take them from the mass media and from gangs. Radio and television heroes, with their copies among neighborhood gangs, now play a vital part in the socialization process. Parents have an uphill and none too successful struggle against these sources. Like adult mobs, children's groups readily adopt the sensational, the cruel, and the most easily understood for their models and standards. These influences then corrupt and lower adult standards, as parents become increasingly afraid to assert their own authority for fear of turning out "maladjusted" children.*

The mass media have largely succeeded in battering down the walls of the social cell the family once constituted in the larger structure of society. Privacy has greatly diminished. Newspapers, radios, and television have very largely destroyed the flow of private communications within the family that were once the basis of socialization. Even meals are now much less of a family affair. Small children are frequently plumped down in front of the television set with their supper on a tray before them to keep them quiet. Since

---

* It is sometimes claimed that the modern family still represents a bulwark against mass and totalitarian pressures. No doubt this is true in the best cases, those few where parents are still able to combine authority and affection. These are, however, mainly a relic of Victorian times. By and large it seems more likely that the family constitutes the "transmission belt" through which totalitarian pressures toward conformity are transmitted to the parents through the influence of the children.

the family does less as a unit, genuine emotional ties among its members do not spring up so readily.[5] The advertising campaign for "togetherness" provides rather concrete evidence that family members would rather not be together.

The mother, at least in American society, is generally supposed to be the homemaker and the center of the family. Has she been able to take up the slack produced by the change in the father's role? Is she, perhaps, the happy person whose face smiles at us from every advertisement and whose arts justify the sociologists' case? A more accurate assessment may be that the wife suffers most in the modern middle-class family, because the demands our culture puts upon her are impossible to meet. As indicated by advertisements, fiction, and even the theories of sociologists, the wife is expected to be companion, confidante, and ever youthful mistress of her husband.

If the demands could be met, many wives might feel very happy in this fulfillment of their personality. The actual situation is very different. The father is out of the house all day and therefore can be neither overlord nor companion. With the father absent, radio and television provide the mother with a watery substitute for adult companionship. A young colleague told me recently that his wife leaves the radio on all day merely to hear the sound of a grown-up voice. The continual chatter of little children can be profoundly irritating, even to a naturally affectionate person. The absence of servants from nearly all American middle-class households brings the wife face to face with the brutalizing features of motherhood and housework. If she had the mentality of a peasant, she might be able to cope

with them more easily. Then, however, she could not fulfill the decorative functions her husband expects. As it is
now, diapers, dishes, and the state of the baby's bowels absorb the day's quota of energy. There is scarcely any strength
left for sharing emotions and experiences with the husband,
for which there is often no opportunity until the late hours
of the evening. It is hardly a wonder that the psychiatrists'
anterooms are crowded, or that both husband and wife seek
escapes from psychological and sexual boredom, the cabin
fever of the modern family. For the wife, either a job or
an affair may serve equally well as a release from domesticity.

A further sign of the modern family's inadequacy in
stabilizing the human personality may be seen in the
troubled times of adolescence. This stage of growing up has
been interpreted as a rejection of adult standards of responsibility and work by youngsters who are about to enter adult
life. It seems to me that this period is more significantly one
of pseudo-rebellion, when the youngsters copy what they
see to be the real values of adult life instead of the professed
ones. Even in the more extreme forms of youthful rebellion,
relatively rare among respectable middle-class children, such
as roaring around in noisy cars to drinking and seduction
parties, the adolescents are aping actual adult behavior.
Adolescents then do things they know many grown-ups do
when the latter think they are escaping the observant eyes of
the young. A "hot-rod" is, after all, nothing but an immature
Cadillac. Where the Cadillac is the symbol of success, what
else could be expected? Adult standards too are made
tolerable through commercialized eroticism that lures us
on to greater efforts and greater consumption from every

billboard and magazine cover. Thus the whole miasma of sexual and psychological boredom in the older generation, pseudo-rebellion and brutality in the younger one, is covered over by a sentimental and suggestive genre art based on commercial sentiment.

No doubt many will think that these lines paint too black a picture. Statistics could perhaps be accumulated to show that families such as the type sketched here are far from a representative cross-section of American middle-class life. Such facts, however, would not be relevant to the argument. As pointed out elsewhere in these essays, the representative character of certain types of social behavior is not necessarily relevant to estimates of current and future trends. This kind of statistical defense of the status quo represents that of a certain maiden's virtue by the claim, "After all, she is only a little bit pregnant."

To refute the appraisal offered in these pages it would be necessary to demonstrate that they misrepresent basic structural trends in the family in advanced industrial countries. The most important argument of this type that I have encountered asserts that the proportion of married people in the population has steadily risen while the proportion of single individuals has steadily dropped. Therefore, people obviously prefer family life to bachelorhood, and the gloomy picture sketched above must be nothing more than vaporings of sour-bellied intellectuals thrown on the dumpheap by the advance of American society.

Before discussing the question further, let us look at some of the relevant facts. The table below shows changes in the proportions of single, married, and divorced persons in the United States from the age of fourteen onward. The source, an authoritative and very recent statistical survey of the American family, has standardized the proportions for age, using the 1940 age distribution as a standard, in order to eliminate changes due merely to shifts in the age composition of our population, which would merely confuse the issue.[6]

Percentage distribution of persons 14 years and over by marital status and sex in the civilian population
1890–1954

Year	Male			Female		
	Single	Married	Divorced	Single	Married	Divorced
1954	28.4	66.7	1.8	22	65.8	2.2
1950	29.4	65.5	1.5	22.5	64.8	2.1
1940	34.8	59.7	1.2	27.6	59.5	1.6
1930	34.7	59.1	1.1	26.9	59.7	1.3
1890	36.7	57.9	0.2	27.8	57.7	0.4

The figures do show a rise in the proportion of married persons and a decline in the proportion of single ones. They also show that the proportion of married persons is overwhelmingly larger than the number of divorced ones. But the biggest change has been in the proportion of divorced people. For men it has risen ninefold since 1890 and for women more than fivefold. A bigger proportion of people are married now than in 1890, but a *much* bigger proportion have abandoned the marital state. In the long run, the latter change might turn out to be the more important one.

Even the statistical evidence, in other words, does not uphold in a completely unambiguous manner the sociologists' argument for the family. Sometimes an attempt to save the case is made by interpreting the rise in divorce as something that allows greater freedom for the individual to choose marital partners on the basis of congeniality. Thereby divorce allegedly strengthens the family's function as a source of emotional support.[7] By talking about greater freedom for the individual in this fashion one has already taken a long step toward the opponents' view that marriage as such may be superfluous.

The point cannot be considered merely in the light of the facts as they exist now or have existed in the past. To do this in social questions is basically unscientific. Those who dismiss negative appraisals of the family with the crude observation that they reflect personal bias or mere "European decadence" deserve an equally crude reply: "So what if Americans prefer to get married! That simply shows how stupid they are."

Acrimony here unfortunately conceals a genuine issue. It is perfectly possible that conditions exist, perhaps even now, that permit better institutional arrangements than most people would be willing to accept. The word better, of course, implies a definite standard of judgment. One can debate such standards endlessly, and perhaps cannot reach agreement without at some point making arbitrary assumptions. I shall not enter this debate here except to say that any social institution is a bad one that imposes more suffering on people than is necessary when they have sufficient material resources and scientific knowledge to do away with this suffering. This standard, anthropologists tell us, is that not only of Western culture, but of all culture.[8]

What then, are the prospects for the future? We need not

take a completely determinist view. Indeed, the perceptions that both plain people and opinion makers have about the present enter in as a significant component among the forces shaping the future and thereby provide an entering wedge for rational adaptation.

Among those who accept a substantial part of the preceding image of the family as basically correct, one frequently hears the prescription that what American culture really needs is a higher evaluation of the social role of the housewife and of motherhood. The trouble with this prescription, I would suggest, is that it merely increases the element of self-deception already so prevalent in our culture. Under present conditions motherhood *is* frequently a degrading experience. There is nothing to be gained by concealing the facts in the manner of an advertising campaign designed to raise the prestige of a particular occupation. We would not think of trying to eliminate the hazards of coal mining in this way. Why should we try to do it with motherhood? If it is true that under present circumstances the experience of motherhood narrows and cramps the personality rather than promotes the development of its capacities, some other way will have to be found if it is to be a real solution.

The trend towards a continually more efficient technology and greater specialization, which dominates the rest of our culture, may conceivably provide an answer. In regard to the division of labor it is important to recall one widely known but neglected fact. In the past, whenever human beings have acquired sufficient resources and power, as among aristocracies, they have put the burden of child-rearing on other shoulders. Twenty years ago Ralph Linton pointed out that "aristocrats the world over . . . are reluctant to take care of their own children. Anyone who has had to take care of two or three infants simultaneously will understand why. This arduous business is turned over to slaves or servants. . . ." [9]

Since the decline of slavery, a basic trend in European society has been to transfer to machines more and more tasks formerly carried out by slaves. By and large, this change has been accompanied by the growth of large organizations to perform tasks formerly scattered among many small groups. This trend may well affect the family. Specialized human agencies, developing from such contemporary forms as the crèche, play school, and boarding school, might assume a much larger share of the burden of child rearing, a task that could in any case be greatly lightened by machinery for feeding and the removal of waste products. Can one sensibly argue that the technical ingenuity and resources required to solve this problem are greater than those necessary for nuclear warfare? Are we to regard as permanent and "natural" a civilization that develops its most advanced technology for killing people and leaves their replacement to the methods of the Stone Age?

Against this viewpoint it is usually argued that human infants require some minimum of human affection, even fondling, if they are to survive, and that therefore some form of the family is bound to remain. The premises may be correct, but the conclusion does not follow. A nurse can perform these tasks of giving affection and early socialization just as well as the parents, often better. The argument does not prove anything therefore about the inevitable necessity of the family.

At the same time this point of view does call attention to certain important problems. Industrial society is not likely to produce household nurses, or any form of "servant class" in abundance. On the other hand, as everyone knows who has been in a hospital, nurses in a bureaucratic setting have a strong tendency to treat persons under their care "by the book," without much regard for their individual tasks and requirements. This is a well-known trait of bureaucracy, which tends to treat people and situations alike in order to achieve precision and efficiency. Infants and small children on the contrary require individual attention. For some years they may need to feel that they are the center of the universe. How then can the characteristics of bureaucracy be brought in line with those of maternal affection?

Though this may be the most difficult problem facing any qualitative transformation of the family, it is not necessarily insoluble. In the first place, as Bertrand Russell points out, a good institutional environment may be better for the development of the human personality than a bad family one.[10] In the second place, an increase in the resources allocated to a bureaucratic organization can greatly increase its flexibility and capacity to satisfy variations in individual temperament. Any first-class hotel knows how to cope with this problem. In a few of the best ones in Europe the guest can have privacy and the illusion of being the center of the universe. Finally, one might legitimately expect that the persons who are drawn to serve in any such child-rearing institutions of the future would have more than the average amount of fondness for children, as well as general human warmth and kindliness. Under proper circumstances and management such institutions could give full scope to these benevolent sentiments.

Certain other considerations suggest an alternative that has at least the merit of being much more palatable to the vast majority of people today, since it is more in line with our deep-rooted cultural traditions. These considerations are essentially two. One is the possibility of some innate biological trait roughly resembling the "maternal instinct." The other lies in technological developments that might allow for wider dissemination of machinery to lighten household tasks and to take over the more routine aspects of child rearing. The dish-washing machine, laundromat, and, as a much more extreme device, the "Skinner box" represent prototypes of this technological development that could strengthen decentralized arrangements for rearing children.

I do not know what students of human physiology now believe about the maternal instinct. Common observation is enough to show that it cannot be an instinct like sex or hunger. There are many women who never become fond of children, or who soon cease to be fond of them. For them the institutional outlet just sketched would be the most satisfactory way of providing for their offspring. But for others, possibly the majority, the gestation period with its trials and burdens may be enough to create in the mother a desire to retain the infant under her care, after which she could become reluctant to give it up. If machinery were available to lighten child-rearing and household tasks on a far wider scale than is now the case, mothers might be able to satisfy the more positive desires of motherhood. One that seems to be quite important in the middle class is the desire to mold the child according to some ideal image, though it is now contradicted by fears of damaging the child that derive from superficial popularizations of Freud.

For the home to become again the place where human beings take the first important steps toward realizing their creative potentialities, parents would have to become willing once more to assert their authority. In turn this authority would have to acquire a rational and objective basis, freed of current attempts to revive religious taboos. Thus there would have to be a philosophical as well as a social revolution whose implications we cannot here pursue. One aspect, nevertheless, deserves to be stressed. Rational arguments can be given only to persons competent to understand them. For obvious reasons children are not able to absorb all rational arguments at once, though the present system of education undoubtedly postpones the development of this faculty where it does not destroy it altogether. Therefore parents will have to learn not to be afraid of saying to a child, "You are not old enough yet to understand why you have to do this. But you must do it anyway." The "progressive" family, where every decision turns into an incoherent and rancorous debate, actually contributes to reactionary tendencies in society by failing to equip the next generation with adequate standards of judgment.

There are, however, some grounds for doubting that this conservative solution will eventually prevail as the dominant one. The disappearance of the wider economic functions of the family would make it very difficult, and probably impossible, to restore the emotional atmosphere of a cooperative group in which the father has a respected authority. Furthermore, the bureaucratic division of labor has proved the most effective way of solving recurring and routine problems in other areas of life. Though a considerable part of the task of raising children is not routine, a very great portion is repetitive. For these reasons one may expect that semi-bureaucratic arrangements will continue to encroach on the traditional structure of the family. No doubt many individual variations, combinations, and compromises will remain for some time to come. Yet one fine day human society may realize that the part-time family, already a prominent part of our social landscape, has undergone a qualitative transformation into a system of mechanized and bureaucratized child rearing, cleansed of the standardized overtones these words now imply. As already pointed out, an institutional environment can be warm and supporting, often warmer than a family torn by obligations its members resent.

Such a state of affairs, if it comes at all, is well over the visible horizon now. Quite possibly it may never come at all. If it does come, there is not the slightest guarantee that it will solve all personal problems and land us in a state of air-conditioned euphoria. Values that many people hold high today may go by the board, such as the affection older couples show for one another who have shared the same pains in life until they have grown but a single scar. It is also possible that a world of reduced family burdens might be one of shallow and fleeting erotic intrigues, based really on commercial interests.[11] Hollywood could conceivably be the ugly prototype of such a future world, especially in its earlier transitional phases. The most that might be claimed by any future apologist for such institutions, if they ever come to pass, is that they gave greater scope to the development of the creative aspects of the human personality than did the family, which had begun to damage rather than develop this personality under advancing industrialism. And the most that can be claimed for the arguments supporting this possibility is that they correspond to some important trends visible in the family itself as well as in the rest of society. Nevertheless, it would appear that the burden of proof falls on those who maintain that the family is a social institution whose fate will differ in its essentials from that which has befallen all the others.

· 6 ·

REFLECTIONS ON CONFORMITY
IN INDUSTRIAL SOCIETY

In everyday conversation the word conformity carries unpleasant connotations. It suggests uniformity, mediocrity,
regimentation, moral cowardice, repression — all the ugly
traits that some thoughtful people regard as the stigmata of
advanced industrial society. These emotional overtones can
blind us to important problems. Chief among them is one
that arose at the end of the discussion of the connection between industrialism and totalitarianism. How can one
separate valid social criticism from mere romantic nihilism?
In other words, do we really want a society completely
without conformity? Is such a society either desirable or
possible? What kinds and degrees of conformity might remain necessary even under the optimistic assumption that
industrial society will develop in such a way as to maximize
human freedom?

The condemnation of conformity stems from a powerful
and valuable tradition in Western culture, one that often
takes a pessimistic view of the present in order to high-
light optimistic possibilities for the future. This trait may be

one of the most significant sources of dynamism in Western civilization. Among its recent expressions I should like to draw attention to the stimulating and generally persuasive view of repression in modern "democratic" society that Professor Herbert Marcuse presents in his book *Eros and Civilization,* along with a somewhat less convincing image of eventual liberation. In less capable hands, however, this tradition becomes sheer utopianism about the future and mere peevishness about the present. When that happens, the cause of tyranny is the only one to profit.

How, then, are we to distinguish between valid critical insights and a purely vicious and destructive attitude toward our society and its institutions? Many people can sense intuitively the difference between the two viewpoints. Intuition is of course not enough. We must go farther. We must try to discover some firm basis for judgment. If we knew something about the minimum content of conformity necessary to make an industrial society work, we should have at least a reasonably firm basis for such distinctions. For the sake of discussion we can accept the desirability of the optimists' goals and even give them the benefit of the doubt on certain points regarding the feasibility of these goals. To do this may help the discussion to move forward toward a discovery of the limits of the optimistic argument. To accept their premises provisionally in an attempt to discover the limits of their argument does not compel us to believe that industrial society will actually develop along the path projected by the optimists. To agree that something is possible is not the same thing as to say that it is probable. For the time being we can set aside any questions about the probable future of industrial society.

To make a convincing case about the minimum of conformity in industrial society requires knowledge about the historical sources of present-day conformity. Some tentative observations are offered in "Totalitarian Elements in Pre-industrial Societies." Without an adequate understanding of its causes we are not in a position to say what aspects of contemporary conformity are excessive and what aspects are essential for preserving and extending those features of modern life, perhaps best summed up as the conquest of nature, that represent preliminary conditions for the liberation of man. Here it is only possible to suggest that some of the generally accepted answers may not be the correct ones and to hint at alternative lines of inquiry.

The widely stressed connection between conformity and modern mass production, with its standardization of jobs, artifacts, and styles of life, is at best problematical. Much evidence shows that peasants in pre-industrial society were just as subject to the crushing burden of custom — and as little aware that the burden was a crushing one — as the majority of the inhabitants of an American suburb are today. Perhaps the sources of pressure toward conformity have changed more than the degree of conformity itself. With the growth of mass entertainment and mass culture out of mass production, diffuse social coordination through the mores may have given way to consensus that is engineered and created at a few crucial points. About even this change we cannot be absolutely certain. The notion of a passive manipulable mass has probably been overdone. It is by no means clear who does the manipulating. In the United States, at any rate, the producers of mass entertainment make every effort to "give the people what they want" and are penalized through the box office and the advertising sponsor when they deviate from popular taste. It might be more correct to assert that both the manipulators and the manipulated are prisoners of a larger field of forces which both create and from which neither one can escape. This judgment may apply equally to totalitarian dictators, who must work through specific sections of the population which for reasons of their own are willing to support the aims of the dictatorship.

Too much may also have been made of the notion that an authoritarian family structure produces and supports an authoritarian political regime, while a milder system of authority in the family is supposedly associated with democracy. The late Franz Neumann has dropped a hint to the effect that the opposite relationship may hold true. As parents bring up their children in a "permissive" atmosphere, they may fail to equip them with adequate moral and intellectual standards. For this reason the youth readily falls prey to any demagogue who offers simple explanations and pseudo-certainty in a complex and uncertain world.

Toward a positive answer concerning the sources of modern conformity de Tocqueville offers many suggestive insights, which, in my judgment, are worth pursuing. As is well known, he saw many of the difficulties of democracy as the consequence of a uniformity inherent in the ideal of social equality. This ideal long antedates the use of machinery in industry on any wide scale, though the two may of course be connected as the double product of some larger cultural trend. In America and England, as we reduce economic inequalities and privileges, we may also eliminate the sources of contrast and discontent that put drive into genuine political alternatives. In the United States today, with the exception of the Negro, it is difficult to perceive any section of the population that has a vested material interest on behalf of freedom. Certainly there is nothing that corresponds to the emerging middle class that opposed both the remnants of feudalism and royal autocracy in England during the late eighteenth and early ninteenth centuries. With its rough counterpart in France, and drawing to its cause eminent thinkers from widely different walks of life, this class gave us the intellectual heritage that has in our time deteriorated into the advertising slogans of the expert in psychological warfare. There is, I think, more than a dialectical flourish in the assertion that liberty requires the existence of an oppressed group in order to grow vigorously. Perhaps that is the tragedy as well as the glory of liberty. Once the ideal has been achieved, or is even close to realization, the driving force of discontent disappears, and a society settles down for a time to a stolid acceptance of things as they are. Something of the sort seems to have happened to the United States. On the international scale this is still very far from the case.

With these very tentative suggestions we must turn to our central problem, the kinds and degrees of conformity required by industrial society. For the sake of discussion let us assume that the process of mechanization and automation will in time embrace all the major sectors of the economy. This would mean that the type of repressive coordination necessary to supply humanity with material goods would have disappeared. Never again would men have to suffer as in the building of the pyramids.

Does the disappearance of toil and scarcity imply the disappearance of repressive conformity? As the example of the pyramids recalls at once, by no means have all the repressive dominations in history been organized as a response to scarcity. To trace all past repression either directly or indirectly to scarcity is a naive oversimplification. Therefore the prospect of the elimination of scarcity should not make us jump to optimistic conclusions about the freedom that this change could bring. The elimination of toil through technological advance is certainly one essential prerequisite for human freedom. But, as the French are fond of reminding us, technological advance is not the same thing as freedom. Nor do I see any trustworthy guarantee that by itself it will bring about freedom. Revolutions, yes, but not necessarily freedom. If scarcity is not the only source of repressive conformity and technical progress alone is no guarantee of liberty, it follows that the elimination of scarcity would remove only certain sources of conformity, while others might easily remain.

Before pursuing this point further it is well to pause and consider one common objection to this whole line of reasoning. It is often claimed that scarcity can never be eliminated because human wants are inherently unlimited. This argument is not convincing. If human wants were essentially unlimited, it is highly unlikely that modern society would have developed the whole apparatus of advertising to create more and more wants. Furthermore, at the level of straightforward biological needs, such as those of sleep, food, and sex, there is an obvious upper limit of satiation. More subtle cultural and psychological needs, such as those for affection and admiration, do not have such clear upper limits. On the other hand, these vary with changing historical conditions. How they will be affected by the future of industrial society is an open question to which both pessimistic and optimistic answers are possible.

However, it is necessary to make clear what is meant by the elimination of scarcity. Quite emphatically it does not mean a television set in every room, or more generally, a superabundance of gadgets. By itself an increase in gadgets would merely intensify scarcity by increasing our intellectual starvation. Such a solution is like forcing water and sawdust down the throat of a man dying of hunger. The elimination of scarcity instead means the creation of a situation in which it is possible for people to escape routine and deadening toil (but not the more challenging and interesting kinds of work), to satisfy biological needs, and to develop those creative capacities that distinguish humanity from the beasts.

There are other and more cogent reasons for believing that many kinds of conformity will remain necessary features of human society under even the most advanced technology. If we set aside the kind of conformity that arises out of toil, or even the whole productive ethic of modern industrialism, some of the more important remaining kinds might be grouped under five rough-and-ready empirical headings.

The first and most obvious is conformity with the basic logical principles of the world around us. Two times two makes four no matter how much or how little labor we have to perform. There is conformity and no little pain in learning such principles. Even if some philosophers tell us that in doing this we are only learning the glories of the human mind and that the universe is nothing more than a mind which transcends our limited faculties, there is still the element of conformity to basic principles which exist as something real outside our finite human organisms.

A second basis of conformity stems from the simple fact that the achievements of human culture require effort and discipline, not only to create them, but merely in order to appreciate them. This statement holds whether culture is defined broadly with the anthropologists to include all forms of learned behavior, or in the narrower popular sense, limited to the appreciation of certain artistic and other intellectual attainments. How can one fully appreciate a poem by Sappho without going through the drudgery of learning Greek? How can one learn the joys of friendship without some elementary curbing of egotistical impulses? Moreover, to create new and further cultural achievements for mankind will probably always be a task reserved for the few with superior talents. This is a task that requires in most cases even greater self-discipline than in learning — and is often the outcome of intense personal suffering.

In the third place, the elimination of routine and toilsome

tasks from the economy through the continued advance of mechanization will not eliminate the need for managerial decisions. Some way will still have to be found to answer certain basic questions confronting any industrial society. These questions constitute the core of classical economic analysis. They may be formulated as 1) what goods shall be produced, the familiar guns versus butter question; 2) how may resources be combined most efficiently to produce them; 3) how will the products be allocated among the population, or who is to get what; and 4) what proportion of resources will be set aside to replace worn-out machinery and for new construction. For these decisions to be made smoothly there must be some method of reaching peaceful agreement. Any such method implies the existence either of a universally accepted criterion for making "good" decisions, or else a series of techniques, that can vary from majority rule to the use of storm troopers, for reaching some decision that can be carried out. In any conceivable case, human beings must continue to conform to some pattern of economic decisions.

It is possible to extend this type of analysis to other social institutions, such as the family. Here the going becomes more treacherous. As pointed out in the preceding essay, most sociologists today believe that something approximating the father-mother-children relationships is a universal social necessity. I see some grounds for doubting this necessity, mainly because I believe that the modern urban family has become a highly repressive institution, many of whose irksome functions could be more effectively and less painfully performed through institutions resembling the nursery and the boarding school. That, however, is a big question that can be no more than mentioned here.

Again without going into specific details, we can say with some confidence that any future society will have to find some way of coping with basically selfish, aggressive, and evil tendencies in biological human nature. How much industrialism, as it continues to grow and develop, may release and intensify these traits remains an open question. There are good grounds for a pessimistic answer. Industrialism could even obliterate the memory of and desire for a world composed of anything except more and more thrills and gadgets. But even if one takes the optimistic view, we cannot safely rule out a certain residue of anti-social propensities in *homo sapiens*.

Finally, all known human societies have shown some attachment to non-empirical beliefs though, if we consider certain subgroups in a society, not necessarily religious beliefs. Even in the freest societies there has been a strong tendency to suppress opinions that ran counter to these beliefs. As an organizing principle, each set of beliefs has in the past provided one of the main bases of social cohesion. Hegel would have us believe that these principles have succeeded each other in a continued progress toward higher principles of freedom. I am unable to accept this argument and fail to see how the Inquisition represents an advance toward freedom over the cosmopolitan tolerance of the Roman Empire. Possibly some form of rationalism, if freed of the limitations of its technicist and materialist bias, might some day serve as an adequate organizing principle for human society. So far, there is still room for a great deal of skepticism on this point.

Would the conformity that results from this group of considerations be repressive? Here is the really fundamental question. The answer is partly, but only partly, a matter of definition. For the sake of simplicity, let us concentrate once more on the economic aspects of the problem and again make certain assumptions that appear to be justified by historical trends. Let us take it for granted that the free market as a source of diffuse, decentralized decision-making continues to decline in importance and that all the managerial decisions mentioned a few moments ago come to be made by some central authority. A Hayek would tell us that this trend automatically results in dictatorship or repressive conformity. One can reply that centralization of decision-making is not the same thing as repression. Indeed, centralization often serves as a device through which people can combine their resources more effectively so that the majority gets more of what it wants. Nobody seriously regards the traffic control officer in a busy airport as an agent of social repression. Yet he makes decisions for all the pilots which greatly improve their chances of landing safely. Not every sacrifice of individual autonomy necessarily means a loss of freedom. Therefore it might be tempting to conclude that conformity under a centralization which accomplishes the purposes that human beings set themselves cannot by definition be repressive. Though such an answer draws attention to an important part of the truth, by itself it is inadequate. For one thing it tells us nothing at all about the very strong possibility that centralized decision-making in the interests of all may turn into repressive despotism. I have not the slightest faith in the benevolent self-restraint of any rulers and accept wholeheartedly the liberal insight that power is the only reliable check on power. The liberal scheme of human affairs requires an approximate balance of competing interest groups in society. Whether or not industrialism contains within it processes that upset this balance is a factual and historical aspect of our question that cannot be answered by the manipulation of definitions. For the past fifty years, the trend appears to have been very definitely in a direction unfavorable to the operation of this balance.

There is still another sense in which we cannot say that conformity which accomplishes human purposes is automatically free of repression. Are we willing to accept *any* purposes? Cannot people sometimes want the wrong thing? Would we call free a society in which a dictator had successfully indoctrinated all of his subjects to march willingly at his orders like automatons? If we are not willing to do this, then what objective criteria are there for rejecting some purposes as bad and accepting others as good? Clearly we are faced with the problem of discovering objective limits to the ideal of tolerance.

An examination of the arguments in favor of tolerance may help us to discover these limits. As I understand them, the arguments are based on two major grounds.

In one set of circumstances we may advocate tolerance out of uncertainty that our opinion, or any single opinion, is the correct one. This is the ground for believing in the free expression of opinion in a scientific debate. Out of the clash of opinions it is hoped that the truth will eventually emerge. Thus the main basis for our belief in tolerance in such circumstances is the fact that we do not at present know any standard that we can apply in order to make a judgment between two opinions. Where we do have such knowledge we do make a decision, or delegate competent persons to make the decision for us. Though every established truth is open for re-examination at any time, under the pressure to act we decide on the best evidence available.

This argument in favor of toleration is essentially a pragmatic one: tolerance produces "best" results, "best" according to some other standard, often a technical and materialist one. It is an argument that was used, when it suited his purposes, even by Stalin in regard to Soviet science. I think it is the main one used in support of freedom in America today. We are accustomed to attribute our material and technological superiority to our "free" institutions.

The other argument is closer to an absolute one. Tolerance in this view is based strictly on respect for the autonomy of the human individual. Closely connected with this ideal is the belief that human variety is in itself something good and that the purpose of society is to facilitate the full development of the varied potentialities of the human being.

From these two types of argument it follows that the principle of toleration does not mean tolerance for *any* act and purpose. In both cases the existence of some standard for judging good and bad behavior and institutions is implied. As we have said, even as we approach an absolute standard of respect for human autonomy, it is only within a certain range that all acts are approved and encouraged. Outside this range certain acts are disapproved or repressed. Greedy persons, for example, would be chastised since their behavior interfered with the autonomy of others. The illustration makes it clear that the standard is derived from the commitment to freedom: we reject institutions and forms of behavior that are incompatible with freedom and its further development. Thus the standard is both relative and absolute. It is relative in the sense that it recognizes variations in time and place, even conceding that certain institutions, such as slavery and the taming of the labor force during the nineteenth century, despite elements of unnecessary cruelty, may on balance be necessary steps on the road to freedom. It is absolute in the sense that we judge from a fixed point, a commitment to freedom. Logically it is of course possible to reject this standard, to say that freedom is bad for humanity. But even the rejection implies some standard.

By this route we come to the familiar conclusion that a commitment to freedom includes a commitment to its opposite in the form of some restrictions on human behavior. Earlier in this essay I have tried to show in concrete if sketchy terms what some of these restrictions are likely to be. Since it is clear that not all forms of human behavior can be tolerated in a free society, some element of repression is necessarily involved. An optimist might counter that reasonable people under appropriate conditions will accept all these restrictions voluntarily. This seems to be the essential content of the famous Marxist phrase about freedom as the recognition of necessity. Certainly there is a fundamental difference between the mature man who recognizes the objective necessity of a certain course of behavior and has the courage to adopt it of his own free will and the childish one who has to be cajoled, manipulated, and occasionally threatened in order to make him do the same things. Nevertheless repression exists in both cases. In the mature man we simply call it self-control. Quite possibly the advance of industrial society may require more of this ancient virtue rather than less. To be sure, there may be less of the self-control now imposed by scarcity. On the other hand, a wider range of material opportunities and temptations may require a stronger exercise of this capacity. Naturally this is no plea for a return to Spartan simplicity, the characteristic battle cry of the reactionary from Cato's day to this. It is a plea for distinguishing between the forms of indulgence that stultify and those that liberate creative human capacities.

The distinction between mature self-control and the childish acceptance of a real or imaginary necessity may also help us to appraise various kinds of political and economic centralization. In the West today there is a strong intellectual current that proposes to preserve and extend democracy "scientifically" by a series of centralized controls that provides the "correct" cues so that the masses engage in the "correct" and presumably democratic behavior. Keynes's ideas about the appropriate fiscal policies to combat a depression have apparently provided a major point of crystallization for this type of thinking, though he might well have repudiated some of its later developments.

As long as it remains at this level, this current of thinking is, in my judgment, essentially reactionary. It shares with the totalitarians the idea that humanity is a mass to be manipulated so far as possible by those who are "more intelligent." Possibly this body of thought could be converted into a step toward freedom with the addition of other ingredients. One would be the familiar view that any centralized government would be a necessary evil, to be kept at a minimum to perform socially necessary functions. Its only justification would be that it left the individual free to decide in a mature and responsible way how to spend his leisure, then presumably the greater portion of his time. As already indicated, the realization of such a program would involve a clean break with mass culture as we know it today.

At the same time there are good grounds for questioning the practicability of any such modification of contemporary liberalism, at least for any foreseeable future. As long as we live in a world of competing states, there is no possibility of relegating the state to the role of a service organization. The whole modern trend is in the opposite direction. How long this trend may last no one can predict with confidence. In fact, a plausible case can be made for the operation of a Gresham's law in politics, whereby repressive political arrangements tend to drive free ones out of circulation. Both domestically and internationally a free society has certain disadvantages in dealing with its enemies. In the long run its superior attractions may win out. But, to refer to Keynes once more, in the long run we are all dead.

A more practical problem remains. From the standpoint that freedom implies a commitment to its opposite, it is fatally easy to jump onto the barricades in full-throated defense of the status quo. As I have tried to show, any such conclusion is absurd. Yet, what do we do now? To be meaningful and translatable into action, a commitment to freedom implies a commitment to some concrete society, or set of social institutions, though not of course a total and uncritical commitment. Which institutions? For an earlier generation, convinced that freedom was the inevitable end product and purpose of human history, the problem scarcely existed. By the logic of history, there simply had to be some place in the world where things were getting better. In the nineteenth century it was easy enough to find such places. They were the most important countries in the world. For many thoughtful people today this answer carries no conviction.

Let us look at the problem from a slightly different standpoint. Today the insistent demand for a commitment — commitment for its own sake — is part of a pervasive totalitarian atmosphere. In my city the trolley cars carry placards urging parents, "Give your child a faith to live by." Apparently any respectable faith will do. Its content does not matter. There is no virtue in this kind of thinking, or in urging a pseudo-commitment to pseudo-freedom wrapped in the cellophane package of a Ministry of Culture or a Madison Avenue advertising agency. At the present time, I would suggest, we have more than enough prophets promising to restore youthful faith and virility to a rather middle-aged creed of humanism and democracy. Spectacles and sharper vision are more suitable to the real needs of middle age. Those who seek no more than to show humanity the truth about themselves may have the most important task today — more important than any decision faced by the statesman or others who lead lives of active responsibility. There are times when action and responsibility are really a form of irresponsibility, a device to escape the painful necessity of seeking and facing the truth. The search for the truth and its proclamation is the proper task of the intellectual, not the lettering of agitational placards if he is in opposition, nor the drafting of memoranda if he is simply "in." In turn, an honest search for the truth inevitably implies some element of reservation, an awareness of the limits to the truth one has discovered as well as the possibility that the opponent may not be altogether wrong. In this sense the spirit of intellectual inquiry is inherently opposed to final and irrevocable commitments.

Though there is hope that industrial society will in the future continue to permit some intellectuals to search for the truth, including some of the more unpleasant truths about his own society, there is no firm guarantee that such will be the case. In the future, as in the recent past, circumstances may arise when the only meaningful act open to the intellectual is to go down with his ship, with all banners flying and steam hissing from the boilers, on be-half of principles about which absolute certainty is impossible. Such acts are rare and require a far greater courage than the blind devotion of a fanatic. They also go against the modern intellectual's entire training, which emphasizes the provisional and tentative nature of truth. As individuals we can only hope that if the test comes, we may be equal to it.

NOTES

CHAPTER 1.

Notes on the Process of Acquiring Power

1. The main modern work to argue this thesis is of course Karl A. Wittfogel, *Oriental Despotism: A Comparative Study of Total Power* (New Haven, 1957). This work became available only at the time of revising this essay. Wittfogel's work has been received with extravagant claims. G. P. Murdock, writing in the *American Anthropologist,* LIX, No. 3 (June, 1957), pp. 545–547, has the following to say: "This is a truly great book, one of the major contributions to the science of man in our time. . . . [It] may conceivably even outrank that of the entire corpus of theoretical literature in political science. . . . It provides for the first time a solid theoretical framework on which the 'free world' might base a direct positive assault on the foundations of Communism and Fascism to replace the unorganized rearguard defense which it has presented for some decades to the ideational attacks of its enemies. The political and social systems of Soviet Russia, Communist China, and recent Nazi Germany fall clearly into the pattern of bureaucratic Asiatic despotisms. Far from representing the emergence of new postcapitalistic configurations, they are obvious reversions to a common precapitalistic political typology. . . ." In the light of such claims, and similar ones (see Richard L. Walker in the *Yale Review,* Summer, 1957), I feel it necessary to make some points that would otherwise seem excruciatingly obvious. Wittfogel's central thesis, taken of course from Marx and Weber, is that under certain historical conditions (specified on p. 12) the imperatives of large-scale irrigation and flood control works produce bureaucratic despotism. Whether or not Wittfogel is right in the detailed application of this thesis to the societies he discusses I do not know. But the imperatives of water control simply won't do as an explanation of the central features of Nazi Germany and Stalinist Russia. Even if we put the best possible face on Wittfogel's argument and regard hydraulic despotism as some sort of an ancestor of modern totalitarianism, his argument throws very little light on why totalitarianism emerges in the era of advanced industrialism. Nor are matters helped much if we generalize from water control to the control of major resources. Wittfogel's work tells us practically nothing about

why this centralized control appears under modern condition. And for that matter, as the case of Calvinist Geneva, discussed in the next essay, shows, major elements of totalitarianism can appear without centralized control of resources.

2. See A. D. H. Kaplan, *Big Business in a Competitive System* (Washington, D.C., 1954), pp. 234–241.

3. Derk Bodde, *China's First Unifier* (Leiden, 1938), pp. 1–2.

4. Some sociologists might object to this formulation, since they regard a built-in set of expectations as an essential part of any institution. Unless we know what to expect from other people, there can be no regularity and predictability in human behavior, they assert. Granting this point, I still think that people may change their ideas before they change the structure of their institutions, as well of course as afterward. Thus there were many changes in ideas and expectations before the collapse of the *ancien régime* in the French and Russian revolutions. Hence the two are separable, not only theoretically but also empirically.

5. Arnold J. Toynbee, *A Study of History,* abridgment by D. C. Somervell (New York, 1947), pp. 190, 336–349.

6. P. A. Sorokin, *Social and Cultural Dynamics* (New York, 1937), III, 196–208. See also *ibid.,* 185–196 for a more general analysis of political centralization.

7. The development of such a doctrine played a notable part in the consolidation of Moscow's power in the second half of the fifteenth century. See V. Kliuchevskii, *Kurs Russkoi Istorii* (2nd ed.; Moscow, 1937), II, 111–146.

8. Hedwig Hintze, *Staatseinheit und Föderalismus im alten Frankreich und in der Revolution* (Berlin and Leipzig, 1928).

9. Max Beloff, *The Age of Absolutism, 1660–1815* (London, 1954), pp. 49–50.

10. See H. G. Rawlinson, *India: A Short Cultural History* (4th ed.; London, 1952), chap. XIX.

11. See T. W. Adorno, et al., *The Authoritarian Personality* (New York, 1950), pp. 675–685.

12. For these developments in Christianity, I have found the following sources to be the most helpful: F. Heiler, *Altkirchliche Autonomie und Päpstlicher Zentralismus* (Munich, 1941); Henry C. Lea, *Studies in Church History* (Philadelphia, 1869); J. Haller, *Das Papsttum: Idee und Wirklichkeit* (2nd revised ed., 5 vols.; Basle, 1951–1953). All references to Haller, *Das Papsttum,* are to this edition unless otherwise noted.

13. Lea, *Studies in Church History,* pp. 232–235.

14. *Ibid.,* pp. 240–243.

15. At the height of papal authority, its arbitrary nature reached the point where the "popes sometimes, in virtue of their supreme authority, granted as a special privilege the right not to be excommunicated without cause" (*ibid.*, p. 403).

16. The entry under "forgeries" in the index of Lea, *Studies in Church History,* occupies a full column of fine print. Concerning the most famous of these, known as the Pseudo-Isidore, which greatly strengthened the power of the pope, Haller remarks that they were "the biggest, the boldest, and the most fateful in their consequences, of any forgeries that have ever been attempted." See his discussion in *Das Papsttum,* II, pp. 54–62. It seems likely that the development of printing may have made this type of deception less easy to perpetrate on a wide scale. On the other hand, it aids in the rapid and widespread dissemination of lies about contemporary events.

17. I take the distinction between the internal and the external environment from George C. Homans, *The Human Group* (New York, 1950), p. 90.

18. Haller, *Das Papsttum,* I, 47–136; Lea, *Studies in Church History,* pp. 104–153.

19. See Otto Hintze, "Wesen und Verbreitung des Feudalismus," *Sitzungsberichte der Preussischen Akademie der Wissenschaften* (1929), p. 323. As the author puts it, feudalism is characterized by a division of state power according to its objects, that is, land and people, instead of according to its functions, as in the modern state.

20. Such behavior was characteristic of the papacy at the height of its power. See Haller, *Das Papsttum* (1st ed.; Stuttgart, 1939), II², 6–7.

21. Henry C. Lea, *History of Sacerdotal Celibacy in the Christian Church* (3rd ed., 2 vols.; New York, 1907).

22. This point is argued much more fully and on the basis of a concrete case in my *Terror and Progress USSR* (Harvard University Press, 1954).

23. The most persuasive exposition known to me is Herbert Marcuse, *Reason and Revolution: Hegel and the Rise of Social Theory* (New York, 1941).

24. James Bryce, *The American Commonwealth* (New York, 1910), pp. 325–328.

25. See particularly Rudolf Hilferding, *Finanzkapital* (Vienna, 1910), Part V, for a penetrating analysis of the factors behind the transition from liberal society to a structure resembling modern totalitarianism.

CHAPTER 2.

Totalitarian Elements in Pre-industrial Societies

1. For a different definition but still similar to the above see Carl J. Friedrich, "The Unique Character of Totalitarian Society," in Carl J. Friedrich, editor, *Totalitarianism* (Harvard University Press, 1954), p. 47; and an extended version in Carl J. Friedrich and Zbigniew K. Brzezinski, *Totalitarian Dictatorship and Autocracy* (Harvard University Press, 1956), pp. 9–10. The authors list six traits or characteristics of totalitarianism which, taken together, define this social form and in their view make it historically unique and *sui generis*. They emphasize that these traits constitute a mutually related cluster and hold therefore that it is incorrect to speak of totalitarianism where only one or a few are present. Though I have used a different approach, I have no particular quarrel with theirs, since the main task of this essay is to discover just what traits are present in certain pre-industrial societies. However, one of their alleged characteristics, the technologically conditioned monopoly of the means of effective armed combat in the hands of the totalitarian party, seems to me highly dubious. For a long time most modern governments, including parliamentary democracies, have had an effective monopoly of armed force. Since the party in a totalitarian state is in effect the government, it is equally incorrect to stress mere party control as the distinguishing feature. In discussing this point with the authors, they have pointed out that totalitarian governments could scarcely arise and maintain themselves without this technologically conditioned monopoly. Though this is true, the monopoly itself still does not constitute a distinctive trait. The difficulty that occurs in drawing the distinction this way reenforces the view that in the twentieth century the distinctions between totalitarian societies and others are breaking down.

2. *Eros and Civilization* (Boston, 1955), pp. 101–102.

3. See the essay "Strategy in Social Science."

4. A typical example is Alfred Cobban, *Dictatorship: Its History and Theory* (New York, 1939), while an important exception is Karl A. Wittfogel, *Oriental Despotism: A Comparative Study of Total Power* (New Haven, 1957), discussed in footnote 1 of the preceding essay.

5. Though the term nonliterate is used instead of preliterate to avoid the implication that these institutions are earlier forms of social development, and thereby conforms to current anthropological usage, I think there are grounds for regarding some nonliterate social institutions as earlier in time and even primitive. The point is discussed in another essay below, "Strategy in Social Science."

6. Eileen J. Krige, *The Social System of the Zulus* (London, 1936), pp. 15–16.

7. According to René Grousset, *L'Empire des Steppes* (Paris, 1948), p. 278, Genghis Khan in 1204 acquired the services of a man who could write in a Turkish tongue to manage the rudimentary Mongol chancellery.

8. *Ibid.,* pp. 290–291.

9. Heinrich Cunow, *Geschichte und Kultur des Inkareiches* (Amsterdam, 1937), pp. 82, 139–140.

10. Hermann Trimborn, "Die Organisation der öffentlichen Gewalt im Inka-Reich," *Festschrift Publication d'Hommage Offerte au P. W. Schmidt* (Wien, 1928), p. 754.

11. William Graham Sumner and Albert G. Keller, *The Science of Society* (New Haven, 1927), IV, 786.

12. *Ibid.,* 726.

13. *Ibid.,* II, 1339.

14. See Kluckhohn, "Navaho Witchcraft," *Papers of the Peabody Museum of American Archaeology and Ethnology,* XXII (1944), No. 2, 60–61.

15. *Ibid.,* 56.

16. Sumner and Keller, *Science of Society,* II, 1336, 1338.

17. See C. P. Fitzgerald, *China: A Short Cultural History* (London, 1954).

18. Wolfram Eberhard, *Conquerors and Rulers: Social Forces in Medieval China* (Leiden, 1952), pp. 10–12.

19. See Wittfogel, *Oriental Despotism,* pp. 315, 325, for his criticism of Eberhard, and pp. 27, 32–33, 164, for his evidence regarding the importance of water control in pre-Ch'in and Ch'in times.

20. H. Maspero et Jean Escarra, *Les Institutions de la Chine* (Paris, 1952), pp. 9–10.

21. Derk Bodde, *China's First Unifier* (Leiden, 1938), p. 1.

22. See, for example, Emil Lederer, *The State of the Masses* (New York, 1940).

23. R. Wilhelm, *Chinesische Wirtschafts-Psychologie* (Leipzig, 1930), pp. 19–21; J. J. L. Duyvendak, trans., *The Book of Lord Shang,* with Introduction and Notes (London, 1928), pp. 41–45.

24. Sources discussed in Duyvendak, *Book of Lord Shang,* pp. 44–46.

25. *Ibid.,* pp. 14, 58.

26. *Ibid.,* p. 48.

27. Bodde, *China's First Unifier,* p. 143.

28. Duyvendak, *Book of Lord Shang,* p. 40.

29. O. Franke, *Geschichte des Chinesischen Reiches* (Berlin, 1930), I, 233.

30. *Ibid.*, I, 240. See also Bodde, *China's First Unifier*, pp. 7–8.

31. Bodde, *China's First Unifier*, p. 143.

32. Duyvendak, *Book of Lord Shang*, p. 61.

33. Franke, *Geschichte des Chinesischen Reiches*, I, 232, 230.

34. Duyvendak, *Book of Lord Shang*, p. 179. For age and authorship of this document see *ibid.*, p. 145 and O. Franke, *Geschichte des Chinesischen Reiches*, I, 217.

35. Duyvendak, *Book of Lord Shang*, pp. 210–211.

36. For precedents see Bodde, *China's First Unifier*, p. 163. The banquet is described in Franke, *Geschichte des Chinesischen Reiches*, I, 247–249, where a full account of the incident may be found.

37. Translated in Fitzgerald, *China: A Short Cultural History*, pp. 144–145.

38. Bodde, *China's First Unifier*, pp. 164–165; Franke, *Geschichte des Chinesischen Reiches*, I, 250.

39. Bodde, *China's First Unifier*, pp. 116–117.

40. Franke, *Geschichte des Chinesischen Reiches*, I, 214–217.

41. Fitzgerald, *China: A Short Cultural History*, pp. 67–70.

42. Duyvendak, *Book of Lord Shang*, pp. 211–212.

43. *Ibid.*, p. 200, see also pp. 207–208.

44. *Ibid.*, pp. 168–169.

45. *Ibid.*, pp. 172–173.

46. *Ibid.*, p. 181.

47. *Ibid.*, p. 177.

48. See *ibid.*, pp. 175–176, for a glimpse of the Chinese situation.

49. *Ibid.*, p. 188.

50. Thus Duyvendak, *Book of Lord Shang*, p. 81, points out that law was not a codification of the people's sense of justice and that the reason for publishing the law was mainly to safeguard the government's power through the law's deterrent effect.

51. See Franke, *Geschichte des Chinesischen Reiches*, I, 216, 221; Duyvendak, *Book of Lord Shang*, p. 278. There is also a universal element in totalitarian practice in that the highest servant of the dictator must be as accessible to punishment as the lowliest citizen. In a modern constitutional state the conception of universal rules goes still further: such rules or laws are binding on the chief executive himself.

52. Duyvendak, *Book of Lord Shang*, p. 208.

53. *Ibid.*, pp. 274–275.

54. *Ibid.*, p. 275.

55. *Ibid.*, pp. 276–277, 279.

56. *Ibid.,* pp. 192–193. See also p. 186.

57. Vincent A. Smith, *Oxford History of India* (2nd ed.; Oxford, 1923), p. 74. The exact dates of his reign are uncertain. W. H. Moreland and A. C. Chatterjee, *A Short History of India* (London, 1936), p. 49, gives 297 B.C. as the most probable date of his death. F. W. Thomas, writing in the *Cambridge History of India* (New York, 1922), I, 473, refuses to give any exact dates.

58. See *Cambridge History of India,* I, 480.

59. *Cambridge History of India,* I, 494.

60. See Radha Kumud Mookerji, *Chandragupta Maurya and His Times* (2nd ed.; Delhi, 1952), chap. 2.

61. D. D. Kosambi, *An Introduction to the Study of Indian History* (Bombay, 1956), pp. 139–140, 150–151.

62. I, 475.

63. V. A. Smith, *Early History of India* (4th ed.; Oxford, 1924), pp. 131–133.

64. See Johann Jakob Meyer, *Das Altindische Buch vom Welt-und Staatsleben: Das Arthaçastra des Kautilya,* aus dem Sanskrit übersetzt und mit Einleitung und Anmerkungen versehen (Leipzig, 1926), pp. 17–26. Most, though not all, of our information on these points comes from the *Arthaçastra,* meaning art of government, usually attributed to Kautilya. I have used the German translation cited above. Ancient Indian tradition, questioned by some scholars, makes Kautilya the minister of Chandragupta, just as the *Book of Lord Shang* is attributed to an adviser of the duke of Ch'in. Though some European scholars place the *Arthaçastra* several centuries later, somewhere in the fourth or fifth century A.D., the major authorities on Chandragupta accept it as a contemporary document. See Smith, *Early History of India,* p. 145; Mookerji, *Chandragupta Maurya,* p. 4; *Cambridge History of India,* I, 467. A recent study, Daniel H. H. Ingalls, "Authority and Law in Ancient India," *Journal of the American Oriental Society,* supplement No. 17 (July–September 1954), p. 38, asserts that the "major portion of the text and certainly the basic theories and attitudes of the text derive from the Maurya empire," though he indicates that some scholars still hold to different views.

65. Meyer, *Arthaçastra,* pp. 14–17.

66. Mookerji, *Chandragupta Maurya,* pp. 52, 158–159.

67. Meyer, *Arthaçastra,* pp. 146–150.

68. Kosambi, *Study of Indian History,* pp. 217–218.

69. Ingalls, "Authority and Law in Ancient India," pp. 39–40.

70. Smith, *Early History of India,* p. 136.

71. Quoted from the *Arthaçastra,* book 11, by Kosambi, *Study of Indian*

History, p. 203. The words in parentheses are apparently Kosambi's explanatory interpolations.

72. Henri Naef, *Les Origines de la Réforme à Genève* (Geneva, 1936), p. 22.

73. *Ibid.,* p. 25.

74. F. W. Kampschulte, *Johann Calvin: Seine Kirche und Sein Staat in Genf* (Leipzig, 1869), I, 14. See also Naef, *La Réforme à Genève,* pp. 23–25.

75. Naef, *La Réforme à Genève,* p. 97.

76. *Ibid.,* pp. 41, 54–57; Kampschulte, *Johann Calvin,* I, 8; Eugène Choisy, *La Théocratie à Genève au temps de Calvin* (Geneva, 1897), p. 1.

77. Choisy, *La Théocratie à Genève,* p. 2.

78. Kampschulte, *Johann Calvin,* I, 97.

79. See *ibid.,* I, book II, chap. IV, esp. p. 154.

80. See *ibid.,* I, 162, 170.

81. *Ibid.,* 150, 152.

82. *Ibid.,* 19.

83. Naef, *La Réforme à Genève,* p. 221.

84. Kampschulte, *Johann Calvin,* II, 284–285.

85. *Ibid.,* I, 118.

86. *Ibid.,* 165–166.

87. Choisy, *La Théocratie à Genève,* p. 15.

88. See Jehan Calvin, *Institution de la Religion Chréstienne:* nouvellement mise en quatre livres (Paris, 1859), book IV, chap. 20, section 16 (vol. II, p. 594 in the edition cited). Fuller discussions of this aspect of Calvinism and its historical importance may be found in Ernst Troeltsch, *The Social Teaching of the Christian Churches,* translated by Olive Wyon (London, 1931), II, 590, 619, 628–630; and in Hans Baron, *Calvins Staatsanschauung und das Konfessionelle Zeitalter,* Beiheft 1 der Historischen Zeitschrift (München, 1924), esp. section ii. Since these ideas became important only later we may ignore them here.

89. Kampschulte, *Johann Calvin,* I, 257.

90. *Ibid.,* 259–260.

91. *Ibid.,* 264.

92. *Ibid.,* 261–262.

93. *Ibid.,* 266.

94. Calvin, *Institution de la Religion Chréstienne,* book III, chap. 21, section 5 (vol. II, p. 245 in the edition cited).

95. *Ibid.,* book III, chap. 21, section 1 (vol. II, p. 242 in edition cited).

96. Kampschulte, *Johann Calvin,* II, 282–283.

97. Choisy, *La Théocratie à Genève,* p. 47.

98. P. Charpenne, *Histoire de la Réforme et des Réformateurs de Genève* (Paris, 1861), p. 446.

99. Kampschulte, *Johann Calvin*, II, 343–345.

100. Charpenne, *De la Réforme et des Réformateurs de Genève*, p. 442.

101. Kampschulte, *Johann Calvin*, II, 356–357.

102. *Ibid.*, 364.

103. *Ibid.*, 364.

104. *Ibid.*, 357.

105. *Ibid.*, 382.

106. *Ibid.*, 380.

107. Kampschulte, *Johann Calvin*, I, 288–289.

108. Charpenne, *De la Réforme et des Réformateurs de Genève*, p. 442.

109. Kampschulte, *Johann Calvin*, II, 357–358.

110. *Ibid.*, 362.

111. *Ibid.*, 360–361.

112. Imbart de la Tour, *Calvin*, translated from French by E. G. Winkler (München, 1936), pp. 82–83.

113. *Ibid.*, p. 78.

114. A. Roget, *Histoire du Peuple de Genève* (Geneva, 1879), V, 57.

115. De la Tour, *Calvin*, p. 77.

116. *Ibid.*, p. 76.

117. *Ibid.*, pp. 81–82.

118. *Ibid.*, p. 79.

119. *Ibid.*, p. 80.

120. Roget, *Du Peuple de Genève*, V, 99. Further cases given pp. 99–103.

121. Kampschulte, *Johann Calvin*, II, 384.

122. Compare *ibid.*, 359.

123. Compare Franz Neumann, *The Democratic and the Authoritarian State* (Glencoe, 1957), chap. 9.

124. For a different interpretation see the works by Friedrich and Brzezinski cited in note 1 above.

125. Compare Heinrich Zimmer, *The Philosophies of India* (New York, 1956), pp. 27–34.

126. Compare Troeltsch, *Social Teaching of the Christian Churches*, II, 620; Calvin, *Institution de la Religion Chréstienne*, book II, chap. 2, section 13 (vol. I, p. 140 in edition cited).

127. Jacob Burckhardt, *Griechische Kulturgeschichte* (Kröner edition; Stuttgart, 1948), I, 218.

128. See Norman Cohn, *The Pursuit of the Millennium* (London, 1957).

129. *Democracy in America* (Vintage Books; New York, 1954), I, 273–275.

CHAPTER 3.

The New Scholasticism and the Study of Politics

1. Princeton, 1952.

2. Chicago, 1952.

3. A logician, such as Hans Reichenbach, however, argues that any proposition is a probability statement and thus comes to the opposite conclusion that some form of the notion of chance has universal applicability. See his *Experience and Prediction* (Chicago, 1938).

4. New Haven.

5. Glencoe.

6. New York.

7. The reader may wish to judge for himself by examining some of the formalist writings that attempt empirical application, i.e., particularly the more factual essays in Parsons, *Essays in Sociological Theory Pure and Applied* (Glencoe, 1949); Levy, *The Family Revolution in Modern China* (Harvard University Press, 1949); or Robert N. Bellah, *Tokugawa Religion* (Glencoe, 1957). Two major defects, in my opinion, run through these works. The first is a form of "reverse Marxism," about as one-sided as the more primitive versions of materialism. It assumes that the impulse behind historical change derives mainly from the value system or ideals of a society. Second is a strong tendency to take such ideals at their face value and treat them as dominant working principles in the society. On the latter point it is interesting to compare Parsons's discussion of medical practice in his *Essays* (chap. VIII) and in his *The Social System* (Glencoe, 1951) (pp. 454–466) with two papers by Oswald Hall, "The Informal Organization of the Medical Profession," *Canadian Journal of Economics and Political Science*, vol. XII, No. 1 (February 1946), 30–44 and "Types of Medical Careers," *American Journal of Sociology*, vol. LV, No. 3 (November 1949), 243–253.

8. *Power and Society*, pp. 190–191.

9. In this connection, see W. W. Rostow, "Toward a General Theory of Action," *World Politics*, vol. V, No. 4 (July 1953), 538–543.

10. "Personality and Social Structure," in A. H. Stanton and S. E. Perry, eds., *Personality and Political Crisis* (Glencoe, 1951).

11. See *The Structure of Society*, pp. 144–148.

12. For a convenient summary of varying viewpoints, see A. L. Kroeber and Clyde Kluckhohn, "Culture: A Critical Review of Concepts and Definitions," *Papers of the Peabody Museum*, Harvard University, XLVII, No. 1 (1952), 115–124.

13. They come mainly though not entirely from the writings of Morris Cohen. See especially his *Reason and Nature* (2nd ed.; Glencoe, 1953).

14. This is, of course, what Hegel tried to show in the famous first chapter of the *Phänomenologie des Geistes* (6th ed.; Hamburg, 1952).

CHAPTER 4.

Strategy in Social Science

1. G. Mosca, *The Ruling Class,* translated by H. D. Kahn (New York, 1939), p. 139.

2. See F. A. Hayek, editor, *Capitalism and the Historians* (Chicago, 1954).

3. Hans L. Zetterberg, review of Joseph A. Kahl, *The American Class Structure* (New York, 1957) in *American Sociological Review,* vol. XXII, No. 6 (December 1957), 768.

4. See his *The Methodology of the Social Sciences,* translated and edited by E. A. Shils and H. A. Finch (Glencoe, 1949), chap. I. The essay cited was originally published in 1904.

5. See particularly his "Entwickelungstendenzen in der Lage der ostelbischen Landarbeiter," originally published in 1894 and reprinted in *Gesammelte Aufsätze zur Sozial- und Wirtschaftsgeschichte* (Tübingen, 1924), pp. 470–507.

6. "Zur Lage der bürgerlichen Demokratie in Russland," *Archiv für Sozialwissenschaft und Sozialpolitik,* XXII (1906), 347–349. German allows very frequent use of quotation marks to indicate skeptical doubt about the meaning of words. In accordance with English usage I have removed all but those which seemed to me most important.

7. *Les Règles de la Méthode Sociologique* (Paris, 1947), p. 56. The work was originally published in 1895.

8. *Ibid.,* p. 60.

9. Translated by A. M. Henderson and Talcott Parsons (Oxford University Press, 1947).

10. See his *Systematic Sociology,* adapted and amplified by Howard Becker on the basis of the *Beziehungslehre und Gebildelehre.* . . . (New York, 1932).

11. *Capital, The Communist Manifesto, and Other Writings by Karl Marx,* edited by Max Eastman (Modern Library; New York, 1932), p. 321.

12. *The Theory of Social and Economic Organization,* p. 424.

13. "A Revised Analytical Approach to the Theory of Social Stratification," in R. Bendix and S. M. Lipset, editors, *Class, Status, and Power* (Glencoe, 1953), p. 93.

14. Talcott Parsons, *The Social System* (Glencoe, 1951), is the leading

statement of this point of view, though the above characterization is, of course, my own.

15. "A process is any way or mode in which a given state of a system or of a part of a system changes into another state. If its study is an object of science any process is assumed to be subject to laws, which will be stated in terms of determinate interrelations of interdependence between the values of the relevant variables." Talcott Parsons, *The Social System,* p. 201.

16. In conversation with the writer more than ten years ago, Professor George Lundberg, the leading advocate of a strict natural science model for sociology, confessed that he was at a loss for a good example of a scientific generalization and was unhappy that the only one he could point to was a rather limited one about migration. See his *Can Science Save Us?* (New York, 1947), p. 41. His remark, as far as I can recollect, was one of the earliest impressions leading me to doubt that the search for scientific laws should constitute the primary task of sociology.

17. Compare George C. Homans, *The Human Group* (New York, 1950), chap. 1.

18. See for example his "The Limitations of Scientific Method in Economics," in *The Ethics of Competition and Other Essays* (London, 1935), pp. 105–147.

19. See the introduction by Philipp Frank, editor, in *The Validation of Scientific Theories* (Boston, 1957), p. viii.

20. C. Kirkpatrick and E. Kanin, "Male Sex Agression on a University Campus," *American Sociological Review,* vol. XXII, No. 1 (February 1957), 53.

21. Here the Oedipus complex come to mind, but there are grave doubts as to its universality. See B. Malinowski, *The Sexual Life of Savages* (New York, 1929).

22. Rather than cite other writers, I will point to one of my own works that displays all the faults criticized here. See my article, "A Comparative Analysis of the Class Struggle," *American Sociological Review,* vol. 10, No. 1 (February 1945), 31–37.

23. M. G. Kendall, *The Advanced Theory of Statistics* (5th ed., Hafner; New York, 1952), I, 1. Emphases added.

24. Franz Neumann, *The Democratic and the Authoritarian State* (Glencoe, 1957), chap. ix.

25. On this ground I disagree with the Hegelian strictures against mathematics presented in Herbert Marcuse, *Reason and Revolution* (London, 1941), p. 144.

26. Paul F. Lazarsfeld in his "Introduction" to *Mathematical Thinking in the Social Sciences* (Glencoe, 1954), p. 3.

27. My own writings came close to taking this position. See *Soviet Politics: The Dilemma of Power* (Harvard University Press, 1950).

28. Compare Talcott Parsons, *The Social System,* p. 481.

29. Ironically enough one of the more cogent presentations of this view comes from a historian. See H. Butterfield, *The Origins of Modern Science* (London, 1949), esp. chaps. i–iv. The idea is implicit in the works of sociological formalists from Simmel to Parsons.

30. H. Rickert, *Die Grenzen der Naturwissenschaftlichen Begriffsbildung* (3rd ed.; Tübingen, 1921), p. 246.

31. See his *Karl Marx* (London, 1938), pp. 73–81, esp. p. 79.

32. Franz Müller-Lyer was the most pronounced advocate of this version of evolutionary theory. See his *Phasen der Kultur und Richtungslinien des Fortschritts* (München, 1908).

33. See Ralph Linton, *The Tree of Culture* (New York, 1955), Carleton S. Coon, *The Story of Man* (New York, 1954), and William Howells, *Back of History* (New York, 1954). All three books, directed toward the general public, express a belief in human progress to date that recalls the tone of Victorian anthropology.

34. See Albert Galloway Keller, *Societal Evolution* (rev. ed.; New York, 1931), and William Graham Sumner and Albert Galloway Keller, *The Science of Society* (New Haven, 1927).

35. Further insight into this process, from a biological standpoint, but with important sociological implications, has been shed by R. W. Gerard, Clyde Kluckhohn, and Anatol Rapoport, "Biological and Cultural Evolution," *Behavioral Science,* I, No. 1 (January, 1957), 14–15. Too technical to summarize adequately here, the point concerns variations in adaptive capacities as related to the environment.

36. E. Sapir, "Language," *Encyclopaedia of the Social Sciences* (New York, 1937), IX, 163.

37. See also Gerard, Kluckhohn, and Rapoport, "Biological and Cultural Evolution," 21, for further implications.

38. G. W. F. Hegel, *Wissenschaft der Logik* (Felix Meiner Verlag; Leipzig, 1948), I, 379–384.

39. Harvey C. Moore, "Cumulation and Cultural Processes," *American Anthropologist,* LVI, No. 3 (June, 1954), 347–357.

40. See also on this problem the recurrence of certain aspects of class relationships discussed by Franz Neumann, *Democratic and Authoritarian State,* especially pp. 250–251.

CHAPTER 5.

Thoughts on the Future of the Family

1. Ernest W. Burgess and Harvey J. Locke, *The Family* (2nd ed.; New York, 1953), p. vii. Though this work bears the earmarks of a college text, it is nevertheless authoritative. Burgess is one of the best known American students of the family.

2. Talcott Parsons, Robert F. Bales, et al., *The Family: Socialization and Interaction Process* (Glencoe, 1955), pp. 9–10, 16–19. In an earlier work, *The Social System* (Glencoe, 1951), p. 156, Parsons raises the possibility of the breakup of the family, mainly to indicate how improbable such an eventuality seems.

3. "Professional Ideology of Social Pathologists," *American Journal of Sociology*, vol. XLIX, No. 2 (September 1943), 165–180.

4. New York, 1929.

5. Compare George C. Homans, *The Human Group* (New York, 1950), pp. 444, 450.

6. The figures used in the accompanying table were adapted from the table in Paul C. Glick, *American Families* (New York, 1957), p. 104.

7. Compare Parsons, *The Family*, pp. 24–25.

8. "No culture places a value upon suffering as an end in itself; as a means to the ends of the society (punishment, discipline, etc.), yes; as a means to the ends of the individual (purification, mystical exaltation, etc.), yes; but of and for itself, never." A. L. Kroeber and Clyde Kluckhohn, "Culture: A Critical Review of Concepts and Definitions," *Papers of the Peabody Museum of American Archaeology and Ethnology*, vol. XLVII, No. 1 (1952), 177.

9. Ralph Linton, *The Study of Man* (New York, 1936), p. 246.

10. *Marriage and Morals*, p. 169. For Russell's qualifications see pp. 219–220.

11. For some suggestive counter arguments to this view, see Herbert Marcuse, *Eros and Civilization* (Boston, 1955), pp. 201–202.

INDEX

(Since this book has no bibliography, the index carries authors' names with references to their works when first cited in full.)